Solid Foundation Sermon Starters

PARABLES & MIRACLES

Blueprints for 30 messages
built upon God's Word

C. Barry McCarty

STANDARD
PUBLISHING

Cincinnati, Ohio

Cover design by Grannan Graphic Design LTD

Interior design by Robert E. Korth

Edited by Theresa C. Hayes and Bob Buller
© 1999 by The Standard Publishing Company
All rights reserved.
Printed in the U. S. A.

Solid Foundation is an imprint from
The Standard Publishing Company, Cincinnati, Ohio.
A division of Standex International Corporation.
06 05 04 03 02 01 00 99   5 4 3 2 1

Contents

PART TWO: THE LESSONS HE TAUGHT

The Day God Sent Us His Picture

Colossians 1:15-20

Jesus' life, teaching, and miracles are God's most exact revelation of himself to us. So when we see Jesus, we see who God is and exactly what God is like.

Jesus pictures God as our Creator, Ruler, and Savior.

I. JESUS IS GOD THE CREATOR.

A. Colossians 1:16 says, *"For by him all things were created:* things in heaven and on earth, visible and invisible, whether thrones or powers or rulers or authorities; all things were created by him and for him."

B. Recognizing that God created the world around us, and ourselves as part of that world, is the first step toward true religion.

C. Jesus came to earth so that we could meet and know our Creator. When he turned water into wine, multiplied the loaves and fishes, or calmed the storm on the Sea of Galilee, Jesus was drawing for us—up close and personal—the same picture that God has been drawing across the canvas of nature since the dawn of creation.

D. When we entrust our lives to Jesus, we are trusting in the Almighty Creator whose eternal plan and power cover all events and destinies without exception.

II. JESUS IS GOD THE RULER.

A. Colossians 1:16-18 reads: "All things were *created* by him and *for him.* He is *before all things,* and *in him all things hold together.* And he is the head of the body, the church; he is the beginning and the firstborn from among the dead, *so that in everything he might have the supremacy."*

B. Just as our world is not self-created, so it is not self-sustaining. Jesus not only created the universe, he also sustains it. He keeps the stars and planets in their courses. He is the power behind the laws of physics. He maintains the delicate balance necessary to life's existence. He literally holds all things together. As the apostle Paul told the Athenians in Acts 17:25 and 28, "He himself gives all men life and breath and everything else. . . . 'For in him we live and move and have our being.'"

C. One of the great puzzles of modern physics is how the positively charged protons in an atomic nucleus can possibly stay together. They are held together by something scientists have called the "strong nuclear force." They know the force exists, they can measure it, and they know it is the strongest force in the universe. But they have no idea as to how or why it exists. For the Christian this physical paradox is no mystery. The universe is held together from the atomic to cosmic level by Christ.

III. JESUS IS GOD THE SAVIOR.

A. Colossians 1:19, 20 states, "For God was pleased to have all his fullness dwell in him, and through him to *reconcile* to himself all things, whether things on earth or things in heaven, by *making peace through his blood, shed on the cross.*"

B. Perhaps Jesus shows us God most clearly as the Savior of the world. Our passage says that Jesus' death on the cross "reconciled" us to God. The word reconcile is one of five key words used in the New Testament to describe our salvation in Christ.

1. Every sinner stands before God as an enemy, but when Jesus *reconciles* you he makes you God's friend (2 Corinthians 5:18-20).
2. Every sinner is guilty and condemned before God, but when Jesus *justifies* you God declares you righteous (Romans 8:33).
3. Every sinner is a slave to sin, but when Jesus *redeems* you he sets you free (Romans 6:18-22).
4. Every sinner stands before God as a debtor, but when Jesus *forgives* you your debt is paid and forgotten (Ephesians 1:7).
5. Every sinner is a stranger to God, but when Jesus opens the way for your *adoption* you become a son (Ephesians 1:5).

APPLICATION

Jesus deserves our worship as the Creator of the universe. Do you worship him? Jesus deserves our obedience as the Great Ruler above all others. Is he the Lord of your life? Jesus is the only one who can forgive our sins, redeem us from hell, justify and reconcile us to God, and adopt us into God's family forever. Is he your Savior?

The Very First Miracle

Luke 1:26-38

In a sense, Jesus' very first miracle was his birth. Not only was his incarnation and virgin birth a miracle, but every detail of Jesus' coming to earth shows God's divine hand.

Jesus came to the right person at the right place at the right time.

I. GOD SENT HIS SON AT JUST THE RIGHT TIME.

A. Luke 1:26 says that "in the sixth month" God sent the angel Gabriel to Mary. The sixth month referred to was the sixth month of pregnancy for Elizabeth, John the Baptist's mother.

B. Galatians 4:4, 5 explains: "But when the time had fully come, God sent his Son, born of a woman, born under law, to redeem those under law, that we might receive the full rights of sons." There was an exact time in human history that God had ordained for the appearance of his Son.

C. When Jesus was born, the time was right religiously, culturally, and politically.

1. The Old Testament had been completed for four hundred years. All the prophecies about Jesus' birth were recorded. The Jewish synagogues that circled the Mediterranean world provided a fertile soil for the birth of Christianity. The breakdown of pagan religion and the moral stamina of Rome had stirred the hope of something better in people's hearts.

2. Just as English serves as the universal language of commerce and diplomacy in our century, Greek was the universal language of the first century. Christians who propagated the gospel during the first several centuries had a common language with those to whom they witnessed and with whom they worshiped.

3. Christians are familiar enough with the dark side of the Roman Empire. But Roman law and order had an up-side for the spread of Christianity. Jesus was born during a time of universal peace. The apostles and early Christian missionaries traveled freely and safely throughout the empire on the magnificent road system built by the Romans.

D. Each of these conditions contributed in some unique way to the spread of the gospel. The angel appeared to Mary at a precisely-timed moment in human history—nine months before God chose for his Son to enter the world.

E. Just as there was a right time for the Lord to enter the human race, there is a right moment for the Lord to enter your life. The Bible says that moment is now. For example, 2 Corinthians 6:2 states, "I tell you, *now* is the time of God's favor, *now* is the day of salvation," while Hebrews 4:7 adds, *"Today,* if you hear his voice, do not harden your hearts."

II. GOD SENT HIS SON TO JUST THE RIGHT PLACE.

A. The angel came to Mary in a specific place, Nazareth in northern Palestine.
  1. The nation into which Jesus was born was not a great military or commercial power. It was insignificant in size and poor in natural resources. But its strategic location made it the crossroads of the ancient world.
  2. Jesus was born in just the right place. God could not have chosen a more strategic location for Jesus' life and ministry or for the birthplace of the church.

B. The Lord also knows your address. He knows not only where you are geographically but also emotionally, spiritually, and financially. He knows every detail of your life. God's knowledge of us is so detailed and his interest in us so keen that even the very hairs of our head are numbered (Matthew 10:30). God is aware of where we are and what our needs are.

III. GOD SENT HIS SON TO JUST THE RIGHT PERSON.

A. In many respects Mary was an unlikely candidate to be the mother of the Savior of the world. Although Mary was a descendant of King David, her family was neither wealthy nor influential. She was probably not more than fifteen or sixteen years old, and while that was a marriageable age, it is hard to imagine her assuming the responsibility for rearing God's Son.

B. But there are several factors that made her just the right person. Mary was a virgin. She was willing to believe in the miracle God wanted to work in her life. In addition, Mary was willing to submit her own body to be used to carry and give birth to God's Son.

C. Mary's virginity not only speaks of her innocence and purity, but also of God's ability to do impossible miracles in our lives.

D. God also has a wonderful plan for your life. Just as he selected Mary for a great task, he has also selected you. You are the object of his personal love and attention, and he has something wonderful planned for you.

CONCLUSION

Just as Jesus came the first time to the right person at the right place at the right time, so he wants to enter your life right where you are today.

A Taste of New Wine

John 2:1-11

Jesus' first miracle, the changing of water into wine, revealed his glory and moved his disciples to put their faith in him. We should have the same response.

Jesus brings a refreshing change to life and religion.

I. JESUS IS A WELCOME GUEST.

A. The setting for Jesus' first miracle was a wedding—one of the happiest times in a family's life. Jesus took part in joyful occasions.

B. Jesus loved people, and people loved him. He was an invited guest at this wedding. He was not a recluse. He went to where the people were, and people obviously enjoyed his company.

C. Being a Christian doesn't mean being a depressing sourpuss that everyone avoids. Joy is a fruit of the Spirit. People who are filled with the spirit of God ought to have "charisma."

II. ALTHOUGH A GUEST, JESUS SETS THE AGENDA.

A. When Jesus' mother, who was also a guest at the wedding, told him they had run out of wine, he responded: "Dear woman, why do you involve me? My time has not yet come" (John 2:4).

B. Jesus' response to Mary teaches us two important truths:
1. Jesus is in charge. Jesus says "my time has not yet come" or similar words five times in John's Gospel. Jesus decides what happens and when.
2. Mariolatry, the worship or adoration of Mary, is wrong. While the Bible pictures Mary as a noble woman and calls her "blessed," it does not venerate her. Mary submitted herself to Christ. The practice of praying to Mary or worshiping her as "the Queen of Heaven" is an error the church fell into long after the days of the New Testament church.

C. We should follow Mary's example by acknowledging that Jesus alone is the Lord. He sets the agenda. We should also remember that while he is not always "on time," he is never late.

III. JESUS CAN HANDLE ANY SITUATION.

A. Jewish wedding feasts usually lasted seven days. In a culture that placed such a high value on hospitality, running out of food and drink for one's guests was a supreme embarrassment. Jesus saved the young couple from disaster by providing 120 to 180 gallons of wine—more than enough for the guests, with plenty left over as a wedding gift.

B. Jesus can meet any emergency. He can do more than we ask. He turns emptiness into fullness and disappointment into joy.

IV. JESUS CAN DO WHAT RELIGIOUS CEREMONIES CANNOT.

A. The water jars Jesus used to perform the miracle were those used in the old Jewish purification rituals. They represented the whole Jewish order of external purification. But Jesus has the power to make us clean from the inside out and to fill us with joy.

B. There are two ways to spell religion: "do" and "done." We are saved, not by our "doing" of external religious rituals, but by our faith in what Jesus has done for us.

V. JESUS SAVES THE BEST FOR LAST.

A. The world offers the best it has first, then once you are hooked things get worse. For example, everyone loves cotton candy. The only problem is that there isn't nearly as much of it as you first think and it doesn't last as long as you would like. Plus, you could never live on cotton candy alone. It offers only a temporary sugar high. The world's pleasures are like that: liquor, sex, money, power—all of these seem fun for a while, but none of them lasts forever.

B. However, the wine Jesus made was far better than the best that had already been served at the feast (John 2:10). In other words, Jesus starts by giving us far better things than the world has to offer, then continues by giving us better and better.

C. The day you become a Christian, Jesus forgives all your sins. You receive his life-giving Spirit. You are adopted into God's family. But even better, Heaven itself becomes your eternal destiny.

APPLICATION

There is a practical lesson in this story. Mary told the servants at the feast to do whatever Jesus told them to do. The servants responded by filling the jars "to the brim." Since Jesus can handle any situation, since he can do what we cannot, since Jesus alone brings joy from disappointment and always saves the best for last, we ought always to do what he tells us.

The Power of His Word

John 4:46-53

No one, no matter how rich or powerful, is immune from personal crisis. Sooner or later we will all face some sort of tragedy that will test both our character and our faith. But like the nobleman in this account, our faith can grow even in the midst of crisis. The truths of God's Word teach us how.

Trusting God's promises can transform crisis faith into confident and confirmed faith.

I. THE NOBLEMAN BEGAN WITH A CRISIS FAITH.

A. The royal official begged Jesus to come and heal his son because the boy was close to death (John 4:46, 47). This man came to Jesus because of a family and personal crisis.

B. Sometimes we have to "bottom out" before we learn what real faith is. For example, the production manager of an oil company was called to inspect a temporary sump with a view to building a regular concrete basin instead. He asked a nearby workman if the bottom of the hole was solid. The latter replied, "Solid as a rock!" The boss, being a man of action, promptly put on a pair of hip boots and waded into the sump hole. To his great surprise, he slowly sank to his waist in the gooey mess, and as he was going down he yelled at the workman, "I thought you said this bottom was solid." "It is," replied the workman, "You just ain't come to it yet."

C. When people come to God with a crisis faith, they often slip away from God after the crisis is past. However, this nobleman's faith grew.

II. THE NOBLEMAN'S CRISIS FAITH BECAME CONFIDENT FAITH.

A. Confident faith comes from taking God at his word. John 4:50 reports, "The man took Jesus at his word and departed."

B. God always keeps his word. Whatever God says, he does. Whatever God promises, he performs. Hebrews 10:23 says, "Let us hold unswervingly to the hope we profess, for he who promised is faithful."

C. The great key to having a confident faith is continually searching God's Word and making a habit of pleading his promises in prayer. The author of Psalm 119:49 prayed, "Remember your word to your servant, for you have given me hope."
1. Are you afraid? Read Psalm 121:7, 8.
2. Do you need forgiveness for sin? Hear God's promise in 1 John 1:9.
3. Are you facing some hardship or opposition? Listen to Romans 8:28, 31, 32 speak of the victory God is ready to give to you.
4. Do you need guidance and strength? Isaiah 58:11 tells what God will do.
5. Are you worried about your finances? Believe 2 Corinthians 9:8.
6. Do you need anything at all? Matthew 7:7-11 states that there is no limit to the good things your loving heavenly Father is ready to give you.

D. Whatever your need, you can find some promise in the Bible suited to it. And whenever you read one of God's promises in the Bible, you can take it back to the great promiser and ask him to fulfill his own word. You will thereby increase your faith even more, as the nobleman did.

III. THE NOBLEMAN'S CONFIDENT FAITH BECAME CONFIRMED FAITH.

A. John 4:51-53 reports: "While he was still on the way, his servants met him with the news that his boy was living. When he inquired as to the time when his son got better, they said to him, 'The fever left him yesterday at the seventh hour.' Then the father realized that this was the exact time at which Jesus had said to him, 'Your son will live.'"

B. Our faith is confirmed when we trust God and he answers our prayers. One of the most effective ways to develop a confirmed faith is to keep a record of our prayers and God's answers to them.

IV. THE NOBLEMAN'S CONFIRMED FAITH BECAME CONTAGIOUS FAITH.

A. According to John 4:53, both the royal official and his entire household believed in Jesus.

B. The good news of what Jesus has done for us must be shared with people we know. Who are you sharing the good news with? What are you doing to be a "bringer and includer" at church?

APPLICATION

Will you study the Bible so that you know what God has promised? Will you take God at his word? Will you trust him fully and completely to do what he says? Will you try keeping a prayer journal to record and remember what you pray and what God answers?

The Great Adventure

Luke 5:4-11

Deep in the heart of every human lies a basic longing for adventure, for a life that offers more than the drudgery of our day-to-day existence. Some people search their entire lives, hoping to satisfy that longing, only to discover when death approaches that their search has been in vain. In fact, only the Christian life can meet our desire for genuine adventure.

Following Jesus is an adventure fraught with danger but filled with reward.

I. THE ESSENCE OF THE CHRISTIAN LIFE IS FOLLOWING JESUS.

A. Luke 5:11 reports that, after Jesus' miracle, his disciples "pulled their boats up on shore, left everything and followed him." These first followers of Jesus (and later all Christians) were called "disciples." The word disciple means "a pupil, a learner, one who directs his mind toward some purpose or goal."

B. Following Jesus requires a lifetime of learning and obeying his word. Jesus himself said, "If you hold to my teaching, you are really my disciples. Then you will know the truth, and the truth will set you free" (John 8:31, 32).

II. FOLLOWING JESUS WILL MAKE YOU A FISHER OF MEN.

A. In Luke 5:10, Jesus told his fishermen-disciples, "From now on you will catch men." On this day Jesus filled Peter's nets with fish, but after Jesus' resurrection, Peter would be the first to preach the good news about Jesus and see three thousand people respond in faith on the Day of Pentecost (Acts 2).

B. Just before ascending into Heaven, Jesus gave the entire church his Great Commission in Matthew 28:18-20. The church was quick to follow their commission.
  1. Acts 5:42 says of the first Christians in Jerusalem: "Day after day, in the temple courts and from house to house, *they never stopped* teaching and proclaiming the good news that Jesus is the Christ."
  2. Later, when persecution forced many Christians to flee Jerusalem, "Those who had been scattered preached the word wherever they went" (Acts 8:4).

3. Eventually the early believers preached the gospel to Gentiles as well as to Jews. According to Acts 11:21, "The Lord's hand was with them, and a great number of people believed and turned to the Lord.

III. FOLLOWING JESUS WILL PUT YOU IN DEEP WATER.

A. Jesus told Peter and the other disciples to "put out into deep water" (Luke 5:4). When they followed Jesus' instructions, they caught so many fish that their nets were stretched to the breaking point and almost sank their boats.

B. When we follow Jesus, and especially when we take seriously our call to win other people to him, we will be taken out of our comfort zone.

C. Following God's call to win thousands for Christ will put us in deep water, stretch us to the breaking point, and sometimes make us think we're about to sink. But these are all signs that we are exactly where the Lord wants us.

IV. FOLLOWING JESUS WILL BLESS YOU IMMEASURABLY.

A. Peter, James, John, and Andrew had been professional fishermen all their lives. Yet, Luke 5:9 says they were "astonished" at this catch of fish. Peter was so struck by the power of Christ that he felt unworthy even to be in the Lord's presence. They had never caught so many fish. They had never heard of anyone catching so many fish. It was more than they could ever imagine.

B. When we follow Christ, God supplies our needs beyond anything that we can imagine (2 Corinthians 9:8, 9; Ephesians 3:20, 21).

V. FOLLOWING JESUS IS WORTH WHATEVER IT COSTS.

A. Though the disciples had just received the largest catch of their lives, they walked away from their nets, their boats, their jobs, and everything else to follow Jesus.

B. Jesus said his kingdom was a treasure worth any cost (Matthew 13:44-46). According to church tradition, all of the original twelve apostles except for John died for their faith. Knowing Christ and sharing him with others was a possession so precious to them that they willingly gave up their lives in exchange for it.

CONCLUSION

Will you commit yourself to following Christ with all your heart and to sharing the new life you've found in him with other people? Will you be a "bringer and includer" who continues to make church an open, loving place for new people? Will you pray for and reach out to introduce your friends, family, and neighbors to Christ? Will you give generously of your time, talents, and treasures to accomplish God's vision for your church?

Do You Want to Get Well?

John 5:1-15

While Jesus was in Jerusalem for the Passover, he encountered a man by the Pool of Bethesda, a man who had been lame for thirty-eight years. Thirty-eight years is a long time. It is a long time to be sick. It is a long time to be sick without any friends to help you. This man was not only helpless, he was also hopeless. To understand the truth of this story, we need to note the three things Jesus said to the lame man.

Jesus' healing of the lame man shows how he can bring hope and strength to us.

I. "DO YOU WANT TO GET WELL?"

A. Jesus challenged the man to consider whether he was content with his condition or whether he wanted to be made whole. This is always Jesus' approach. We are free to choose his help or to reject it.

B. Jesus' question also forced the man to admit his helplessness. In John 5:7, the man replies, "I have no one to help me into the pool when the water is stirred." Like the lame man, each of us must come to the point where we recognize and admit that, without Christ's help, we are lost, helpless, and hopeless (Matthew 5:3; Ephesians 2:4-9).

C. Is coming to church simply one more thing on your list of things to do? Is it just one more item on your agenda, mixed in with work, kids' soccer games, and your own leisure pursuits? Is it just another box you need to check off each week because you are a decent person and decent people have to do the "church thing"?

Or do you come to church as a starving beggar who needs the Bread of Life to feed your soul? Do you come as a spiritual blind man who needs to see by the light of God's Word? Do you come as someone who will be lost for all eternity without the mercy and grace of God? Are you willing to admit the desperate condition you are in? If so, then are you ready to receive the healing and blessing that Jesus wants to give you.

II. "GET UP! PICK UP YOUR MAT AND WALK."

A. At first, this seems like a ridiculous command. Jesus was telling the man to do the one thing in the world he could not do. But that is what Jesus does.

He brings us face to face with the impossible, and commands us to act.

B. Jesus' command contained three parts:
1. "Get up!"—Although Jesus had commanded him to do the impossible, there was something in Jesus that convinced the man he could do what Jesus had told him to do. In that moment, when the lame man's will met (and yielded to) the will of Jesus, the Lord's healing power flashed across the connection.
2. "Pick up your mat."—Jesus made no provision for the man to slip back into his infirmity. He would no longer need his mat or his place beside the pool. When Jesus sets us free, we must burn our bridges behind us and cut ourselves adrift from anything that would hold us back.
3. "Walk."—The man would no longer be carried. He would rise up to walk in a new life. God expects us to *do something* with his gifts. We must *use* the abilities he gives us.

III. "SEE, YOU ARE WELL AGAIN. STOP SINNING OR SOMETHING WORSE MAY HAPPEN TO YOU."

A. John 5:3 states that there were a great number of disabled people lying by the Pool of Bethesda. Jesus healed only a single lame man. The main point of the miracle is not Jesus' power over physical disabilities but his power to save us from our spiritual disabilities.

B. Jesus' statement to the man teaches us that there is something worse than physical disabilities: remaining in one's sins. The tragedy of thirty-eight years as an invalid is no comparison to the doom of hell. Though we all would like to have bodies free from defects and disabilities, it is far more important that we have the healing power of Jesus for our souls.

CONCLUSION

Are you willing to admit that you are lost without Christ? Are you willing to "pick up your mat and walk" by repenting of your sins and being baptized into Christ? Are you willing to be set free from the guilt and power of your sins and to live a new life in Christ? Do you genuinely want to get well?

A Soldier's Faith

Luke 7:1-10

This story recounts an unusual event: how a Gentile soldier came to Jesus to ask for the healing of his servant. The centurion was not just a Gentile but an officer in the Roman army that occupied Judea. Centurions were the backbone of the Roman army, generally seasoned fighting men who came up through the ranks to posts of command. But this Roman centurion trusted God and his Word, and that made all the difference for him and for his servant.

God's people need to humbly submit themselves to God and his powerful Word.

I. THE CENTURION WORSHIPED GOD.

A. The centurion came to Jesus through Jewish intermediaries. Ordinarily the Jews would have despised him, but this man appears to have been one of the few Gentiles who worshiped the God of Israel. The centurion even built a synagogue for the Jews in Capernaum. The ruins of an ancient synagogue now standing in Capernaum show Roman architecture with Jewish motifs carved on the stones. The synagogue to which Luke alludes was earlier, but this later one may have preserved something of its style.

B. More remarkably, Jesus announced that he had "not found such great faith even in Israel" (Luke 7:9).

II. THE CENTURION CARED FOR HIS SERVANT.

A. This set him apart from the typical Roman soldier or slave owner of that day, who usually had no more regard for a slave than for an animal. The Greek philosopher Aristotle said, "A slave is a living tool, just as a tool is an inanimate slave." A common saying among the Romans was that the only difference between a slave, a beast, and a cart was that the slave could talk.

B. In Roman law the master possessed the power of life and death over his slave. The centurion was a man's man and a soldier's soldier, yet he had deep compassion for his dying servant.

III. THE CENTURION CAME IN HUMILITY.

A. The centurion sent the Jewish elders to Jesus because he regarded himself as undeserving and unworthy of approaching Jesus personally. Although he possessed power, he bowed before Jesus' greater authority.

B. The centurion also showed sensitivity to the customs around him. Instead of asking Jesus, a Jewish rabbi, to enter the home of a Gentile, he humbly offered Jesus another option.

IV. THE CENTURION BELIEVED IN JESUS.

A. The centurion's initial request demonstrated his belief that Jesus had the power to heal his servant. He had heard about Jesus and believed in the one of whom he had heard.

B. Later the centurion addressed Jesus as "Lord" (Luke 7:6) and then, because he felt unworthy to have Jesus come into his house, said to Jesus, "Say the word, and my servant will be healed." The centurion knew that distance presented no barrier to Jesus' power and authority.

V. THE CENTURION KNEW THE POWER OF JESUS' WORD.

A. The centurion recognized authority when he encountered it, even in a realm in which he had neither experience nor understanding. Soldiers understand what it means to give and receive orders. The centurion knew that, when he issued an order, the men under his command would obey. So he knew that, if Jesus commanded his servant to be healed, his servant would be healed.

B. Because the centurion both recognized and trusted in Jesus' authority, Jesus marveled at the man's faith . . . and healed his servant.

CONCLUSION

Hebrews 4:12 says that "the word of God is *living* and *active.* Sharper than any double-edged sword, it penetrates even to dividing soul and spirit, joints and marrow; it judges the thoughts and attitudes of the heart." The word for active here is *energes,* the root of our word "energy." It describes something that is effective or powerful.

There is a difference between the Bible and all other books. God's Word is alive. It has supernatural power. Therefore, we should:

1. Read it (Psalm 1:1, 2). The average person can read through the entire Bible in a single year by reading only twelve minutes a day.
2. Memorize it (Deuteronomy 11:18-21; Psalm 119:11; Matthew 4:4, 7, 10).
3. Pray it (Genesis 32:9-12; 1 John 5:14, 15). When we use the words of Scripture in our prayers—God's promises, commands, and truths—we can be sure we are praying according to God's will.
4. Do it (James 1:22-25).

The Man Put in His Right Mind

Mark 5:1-20

It is clear from the Bible that there are spiritual beings who have access to the human world and have dealings with human beings. The Bible describes demon possession as a condition in which one or more demons inhabit and gain control over a human being. The personality and voice of a demon sometimes eclipses the personality and voice of the occupied person. Sometimes a demon even makes the person it possesses dumb, blind, or insane.

All this seems strange to us because demon possession is not something we see every day, if we ever see it at all. Reports of demon possession still come from places where witchcraft and the worship of evil spirits is practiced, but it does not appear to be common in places where the church is well established. However, we do know that all the evil around us has its ultimate source in the Prince of Darkness, and it may be that some of what we see today is directly caused by the unseen influence of demons. Whatever you think about that, it is clear that the demon possession we read about in the Bible was real.

The case of the Gerasene demoniac is one of the worst imaginable. The demons had complete domination of the man. In fact, when Jesus asked the man his name, he replied, "My name is Legion . . . for we are many" (Mark 5:9). Although the man answers, he begins by saying "my" and continues by saying "we." The man's voice has become the voice of the demons. Somewhere, somehow, this man had listened to the voice of evil. He continued submitting to the domination of its suggestions until finally he had no will or choice of his own. He was completely dominated by the evil power he had invited into his life.

Jesus has the power to save us from any evil.

I. THERE ARE EVIL SPIRITUAL FORCES IN THIS WORLD SEEKING TO DESTROY US.

A. As fallen angels, demons are powerful beings. They have superhuman intelligence and strength and supernatural powers. Demons also have extensive knowledge of human strengths and weaknesses and have had centuries of experience in tempting people.

B. One doesn't have to be demon-possessed to meet the devil. He tempts all of us, seeking to put us in physical, mental, and spiritual bondage (Ephesians 6:10-12; 1 Peter 5:8).

C. We cannot rule out the possibility that demons still influence people directly today. As our society becomes more secular and the influence of occultism and the New Age movement grows, demonic influences will increase.

II. JESUS HAS ABSOLUTE POWER OVER SATAN AND DEMONS.

A. Jesus mastered the demons who were tormenting the Gerasene man.

1. The demons immediately recognized Jesus, addressing him by name and by title: "Jesus, Son of the Most High God" (Mark 5:7).

2. The demons bowed down before Jesus. When the possessed man saw Jesus from a distance, "he ran and fell on his knees in front of him" (5:6). Although demons hate everything about God, they are powerless to do anything but bow down before Jesus.

3. The demons knew Jesus had the power to destroy them at will (Matthew 8:29).

4. Jesus cast out an entire legion of demons with a single word. Matthew 8:32 records that all Jesus did was say "Go!" to the demons—and they instantly left the man.

B. Jesus is the Master of whatever evil forces tempt and harass us (Colossians 2:15; Revelation 17:14).

III. THROUGH JESUS, WE CAN TRIUMPH OVER THE DEVIL AND HIS EVIL INFLUENCE.

A. Mark 5:15 states that, after Jesus had cast the demons out of the man, he was "sitting there, dressed and in his right mind." Jesus had invaded the demonic realm and completely reversed the evil distortion of the man's personality.

B. Jesus promised us the same kind of powerful help (2 Corinthians 10:4; Ephesians 6:10-18; 1 John 4:4).

IV. JESUS' SAVING POWER MUST BE SHARED WITH OTHERS.

A. Not everyone will be happy when people are saved. When Jesus cast the demons out of the man, the people of the region were afraid and begged Jesus to leave (Mark 5:15-17). Sinful people often react to God's power with fear.

B. The man Jesus delivered from the demons wanted to go with him. But Jesus told him to go home and tell his family and friends what God had done for him (Mark 5:19, 20).

CONCLUSION

Jesus came to save us from sin and to rescue us from spiritual bondage. Through Jesus we can triumph over the devil and share Jesus' saving power with others.

The Miraculous Feeding

John 6:1-15

With the exception of the resurrection, this is the only one of Jesus' miracles that appears in all four Gospels. This miracle took place about one year before Jesus was crucified. Jesus had taken his disciples to the northeast side of the Sea of Galilee for rest. But while they were there, the crowds followed to hear Jesus teach and to have him heal their sick.

Jesus provides more than enough to meet everyone's needs even in an impossible situation.

I. WITH JESUS, NOTHING IS IMPOSSIBLE.

A. In John 6:5, Jesus asked Philip, "Where shall we buy bread for these people to eat?" In verse 7, Philip answered, "Eight months' wages would not buy enough bread for each one to have a bite!" Philip had already calculated the impossibility of feeding the crowd.

B. But verse 6 suggests that when Jesus asked the question, he already knew what he was going to do. He already had the solution to what seemed like an impossible situation.

C. Likewise, in Isaiah 65:24 God says, "Before they call I will answer; while they are still speaking I will hear." You cannot face a problem that God hasn't already figured out. This is why the Bible sometimes speaks of our future glory in the present or even past tense. To God, it's already a done deal (Ephesians 2:4-7).

II. WITH JESUS, NOTHING IS INSIGNIFICANT.

A. Jesus started this miracle with a small boy's lunch. Barley was the grain poor people used for bread. The five "loaves" weren't like our loaves; they were small lunch biscuits. The two fish were dried fish about the size of sardines. It wasn't much, but Jesus fed more than five thousand people with it.

B. Jesus not only fed the crowd until everyone was full, but the boy who gave up his lunch got much more than he gave. He started with a small lunch. He ended up being filled.

C. God often uses small things with greater effectiveness than the things we think of as great and most promising.

III. WITH JESUS, NOTHING IS WASTED.

A. John 6:12, 13 reports that, after everyone had had enough to eat, Jesus ordered the disciples to gather up the leftover pieces so that nothing would be wasted.

B. According to Romans 8:28-31, nothing that happens to us is a wasted experience, for "we know that in all things God works for the good of those who love him, who have been called according to his purpose."

C. Not everything that happens to us in life seems positive or good at the time. Life is often filled with broken dreams and lost hopes. Loss of a job can shatter dreams of financial security, professional advancement, and comfort. A divorce can shatter dreams of home, family, and a loving relationship. A serious illness can shatter dreams of a vibrant, active life full of accomplishment. The death of a loved one can shatter dreams of companionship and years of gracefully growing old together.

D. All of us have dreams, and when those dreams are shattered we are often caught in the morass of disappointment, frustration, and hopelessness. We are a dreaming world of shattered dreamers. So what should we do when our dreams are broken, when our plans fail, when insurmountable barriers stand in the way of our vision for the future?
1. We can give up and say, "It's not worth the effort," and then just do the least that we can with the rest of our lives.
2. We can grow bitter and lash out at God, society, and others, living a life that is sour to us and everyone we touch.
3. We can live in the past, the good old days, and miss God's present (and future) blessing and victory.
4. Or we can dare to dream once again, trusting God to use everything that happens to us for our good. Even negative experiences teach us valuable lessons and shape our character. With God, nothing is wasted.

CONCLUSION

God has a wonderful plan for your life, a plan in which he has already taken care of every "impossible" situation you will ever face. Nothing in your life is insignificant to God—and no life under God's direction and care will ever be wasted.

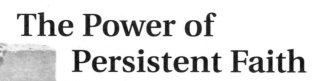

The Power of Persistent Faith

Matthew 15:21-28

Jesus had taken his disciples across the northern border of Israel into Phoenicia for a brief retreat. While they were there, a Canaanite woman approached Jesus with a request that Jesus heal her demon-possessed daughter. This woman was the last person one would expect to come to Jesus. A Gentile, she was outside the privileges of the Jewish race and religion. She had been raised in a pagan culture famous for its wickedness.

When the people of Israel conquered Canaan, God had commanded the army to utterly destroy the Canaanites. The Jews disobeyed that command, and eventually the pagan influences they tolerated were their downfall. But by Jesus' day, the Jews had learned their lesson and had no contact whatsoever with Canaanites. So it is most unusual that this woman would come to Jesus. But in doing so she received a great miracle and taught us a great lesson.

God answers and rewards prayers offered in persistent faith.

I. THE CANAANITE WOMAN WAS DRIVEN TO JESUS BY A GREAT NEED.

A. The Canaanite woman came to Jesus because her daughter was sick. The little girl was possessed by a demon. It was her family's trouble and distress that brought her to Christ.

B. Sometimes it takes some kind of trouble or distress to bring us to Christ. As Mother Teresa once said, "You will never know that Jesus is all you need until Jesus is all you've got."

II. THE CANAANITE WOMAN APPROACHED JESUS WITH GREAT RESPECT.

A. Not only did the Canaanite woman address Jesus as "Lord, Son of David" (Matthew 15:22), she knelt before Jesus (15:25). The New Testament word for "kneel" here is frequently translated "worship."

B. The Canaanite woman also asked for mercy. By definition, someone who asks for mercy asks for something undeserved. One of the fundamental principles of God's grace is that we do not get what we deserve. We get better than we deserve.

C. If you want to know God, if you want salvation, then you must kneel before Jesus, accept him as your Lord, and ask for his mercy.

III. THE CANAANITE WOMAN PURSUED JESUS WITH GREAT FAITH.

A. The Canaanite woman started with four strikes against her. She was a woman, a Gentile, a Canaanite, and a Syro-Phoenician (one of ancient Israel's bitterest enemies).

B. Jesus threw her four more strikes: At first he ignored her (15:23). Then the disciples asked him to get rid of her (15:23). After that, Jesus told her that helping Gentiles wasn't on his agenda (15:24). Finally, Jesus told her, "It is not right to take the children's bread and toss it to their dogs" (15:26).

C. In spite of these barriers, the woman responded in great faith: "If all I can have is the crumbs you'd feed to a dog, I'll take it!" (Author's paraphrase.) The woman pursued Jesus with a passionate, indomitable, persistent faith. She would let no obstacle stand in her way, and Jesus commended her for her great faith (15:28).

D. A helpful acronym to apply to prayer is P.U.S.H.—Pray Until Something Happens. In prayer, as in baseball, stopping at third base adds no more to the score than striking out. When you are waiting on God, it's always too early to quit. Never ever give up.

IV. THE CANAANITE WOMAN RECEIVED A GREAT REWARD.

A. In one of his few long-distance healings, Jesus instantly made the woman's daughter well. The woman's prayers were answered. She received the help she had so earnestly sought.

B. By healing this woman's daughter, Jesus revealed himself as the Gentiles' Savior. While the gospel came through the Jews and to the Jews first, it was never intended to be for them only. As Paul says in Romans 1:16, the gospel "is the power of God for the salvation of everyone who believes: first for the Jew, then for the Gentile."

CONCLUSION

In Jeremiah 29:13 God declares, "You will seek me and find me when you seek me with all your heart." The Canaanite woman teaches us the power of persistent faith. She also shows us that when God delays in answering our prayers for help, he is either proving or improving our faith. God is not always on our schedule, but he is always on time.

Why Do Bad Things Happen?

John 9:1-3

An encounter with a blind man in Jerusalem prompted Jesus' disciples to pose to him one of the most puzzling and often asked philosophical questions throughout the ages: "Why does pain and suffering exist?"

At first it seems the case of the blind man was an easy one to answer. Of course, he was born blind to display God's glory. Jesus was about to heal the man. He would miraculously receive his sight! But what about all the other blind men who would never see? What about the lame beggars who would never walk? the lepers who would never be clean? the grieving mothers who would not receive back their dead children from the grave? What about them?

Though Jesus doesn't heal every case of blindness, as he did this one, his answer to the question gives us a clue to facing pain and suffering in life.

God works everything for our good and his glory.

I. PAIN HAS A PURPOSE.

 A. The pain and suffering we see in the world is the result of human sin. It reminds us that the universe is not "normal," that we live in a fallen and sin-cursed world.

 B. Hard as it may be to believe, pain is often beneficial. Sometimes pain is a spiritual warning that rouses us from our satisfaction and complacency in this earthly life. C. S. Lewis wrote, "God whispers to us in our pleasures, speaks in our conscience, but shouts in our pains: it is his megaphone to rouse a deaf world."

 C. Pain can also be a means to and a sign of growth. Athletes often say, "No pain, no gain." It is through the sweat, strain, and soreness of intense physical training that our bodies become stronger. In the same way, hardship and suffering are also keys to building character (1 Peter 1:3-7).

 D. Sometimes pain and suffering are the price for following Christ. Jesus warned us in John 15:19, 20 that the world hates us because we do not belong to it.

  Clarence Jordan, a minister to the poor in rural Georgia, was getting a red-carpet tour of another minister's church. The minister pointed to the rich, imported pews and luxurious decorations with pride. As they stepped outside, darkness was falling, and a spotlight shone on a huge cross atop the steeple. "That cross alone cost us ten thousand dollars," the minister said with a satisfied smile. "You got cheated," said Jordan. "Times were when Christians could get them for free."

II. EVERYTHING THAT HAPPENS TO US IS FOR OUR GOOD AND GOD'S GLORY.

A. Romans 8:28 says, "And we know that in *all things* God works for the good of those who love him, who have been called according to his purpose."

B. Ephesians 1:11, 12 adds, "In him [Christ] we were also chosen, having been predestined according to the plan of him who works out *everything* in conformity with the purpose of his will, in order that we, who were the first to hope in Christ, might be for the praise of his glory."

C. Helen Keller once said, "Although the world is full of suffering, it is also full of the overcoming of it." By helping us face and overcome suffering and pain, God constantly works for our good and his glory.

III. ONE DAY THE SCALES WON'T JUST BALANCE BUT WILL TILT BEYOND OUR COMPREHENSION TO OUR GOOD AND GOD'S GLORY.

A. We live in a world where God has the last word. It's important always to remember that pain and suffering here are transitory but that the glory God will give us is eternal.

B. Paul reminds us in 2 Corinthians 4:16-18 that "our light and momentary troubles are achieving for us an eternal glory that far outweighs them all." (See also Romans 8:18.)

APPLICATION

We need to keep the right perspective on pain, suffering, and hardship. Our God is faithful. He makes no mistakes. Everything that happens to us who are believers is for our good and his glory—and whatever temporary suffering we may experience, God will have the last word.

The French writer, Paul Claudel, once said that "Christ did not come to do away with suffering; he did not come to explain it. He came to fill it with his presence."

The Resurrection and the Life

John 11:17-27

According to Hebrews 4:15, Jesus, our great high priest, is able "to sympathize with our weaknesses" because he faced every trial and temptation that we could ever face. Nowhere is this more evident than in the account of the raising of Lazarus. Like us, Jesus grieved the death of a friend. But Jesus also looked past that day of mourning to that future day when God will wipe away every tear and fill our hearts with joy that will never end.

Although death is inescapable, Jesus can help us face it today and overcome it in the future.

I. DEATH IS AN INESCAPABLE PART OF LIFE.

A. As Jesus came first to Martha, then to Mary, they each greeted him with the same words, "Lord, if you had been here, my brother would not have died" (John 11:21, 32). Although Jesus possessed and used his power to cure life-threatening illnesses, the fact is that he did permit Lazarus to die. When he first received the news of Lazarus's illness, he waited two more days before coming to Bethany (John 11:6). And even after being resurrected on this occasion, Lazarus still eventually died a natural death.

B. Since the time of the fall, when sin entered God's good creation, death has been a part of life. Only a fool does nothing to prepare for it. Hebrews 9:27 says, "Man is destined to die once, and after that to face judgment." Thus Psalm 90:12 asks God, "Teach us to number our days aright, that we may gain a heart of wisdom."

C. The American magician Harry Houdini became the world's most famous escape artist. He showed astounding ability in extricating himself from handcuffs, ropes, straitjackets, locked trunks, jails, and bonds of any sort. He once had himself tied and then locked in a packing case, which was bound with steel tape and dropped into the harbor off the Battery in New York City. Houdini appeared on the surface of the water in fifty-nine seconds.

But there was one prison from which Houdini could not escape: death. Before he died on Halloween night, 1926, Houdini had promised his wife that he would attempt to communicate with her from beyond the grave. He devised a ten-word code that would authenticate any message he would communicate to her. Every Halloween for the next ten years his wife Bess sat in their home before a candle-lit portrait of Houdini and waited for a signal from him. That signal never came, and finally in 1936, Bess put out the candle and never lit it again. It is futile for even the cleverest and most gifted human being to think he can escape from the prison of death.

II. JESUS KNOWS WHAT IT MEANS TO LOSE A LOVED ONE.

A. Even though Jesus knew he was going to raise Lazarus from the dead, he still wept at the grave of his friend (John 11:35), and those standing by the grave observed, "See how he loved him!" (11:36).

B. It is not uncommon to see someone, even years after a loved one has died, be brought to tears by the mention of that person's name or something else that evokes a memory. While it is true that we need to get on with life after losing someone we love and not be paralyzed by that loss, that is not the entire story. If you love someone deeply, if that person was part of the fabric of your life, then those tears are one of the most powerful ways to say that it was glorious to have loved and to have been loved.

C. When you weep from the loss of someone you love, remember that Jesus knows what that is like. You cannot experience any sorrow that he himself has not also felt and even now feels with you.

D. Jesus also understands what it is like to face one's own death. The raising of Lazarus took place shortly before Jesus' arrest and was the final event that moved his enemies to kill him.

III. JESUS OFFERS ETERNAL LIFE TO US AND TO EVERYONE WE LOVE.

A. This world grasps in vain for some way to escape the certain reality of death. But Jesus has already shown us how to overcome death. The point of raising Lazarus was to show to all that Jesus is the resurrection and the life. He was saying to all who would come to trust in him, "Look, if I can do this for Lazarus now, I can do it for you later."

B. Romans 8:11 promises that "if the Spirit of him who raised Jesus from the dead is living in you, he who raised Christ from the dead will also give life to your mortal bodies through his Spirit, who lives in you."

CONCLUSION

Only Jesus has the power over life and death. His own resurrection from the dead altered the universe forever. He is ready even now to raise spiritually dead people to spiritual life. And he stands ready to raise us all to eternal life when he comes again.

How to Let God Bless Your Life

Matthew 20:29-34

On his final journey to Jerusalem for the Passover, Jesus passed through Jericho. Only eighteen miles east of Jerusalem, it was the home of Zacchaeus, whom Jesus met on this occasion, although Matthew does not give an account of that meeting. Rather, Matthew paints a picture of two blind men who sought and received a great blessing from God, the restoration of their sight. Jesus healed these men because their hearts and minds were ready to receive a great blessing from God.

**God rewards those who commit themselves completely to him
even in the face of obstacles and opposition.**

I. THE BLIND MEN KNEW WHO JESUS WAS.

A. Eight hundred years before Jesus walked through the streets of Jericho, the prophet Isaiah promised that, from the descendants of David, God would raise up a great king who would establish an eternal kingdom (Isaiah 9:6, 7).

B. These men probably didn't understand that the everlasting kingdom Jesus would establish would be the church. They didn't know, and if they knew, they wouldn't have understood, what Jesus was about to do in Jerusalem. Nevertheless, by addressing Jesus as the "Son of David," they showed that they understood Jesus was the Messiah. Jesus was the promised King.

C. The foundational truth of Christianity is that Jesus is Lord, he is the King. If you really understand that, you will eventually understand whatever else God wants you to know. If you understand that, then you have found the path to the blessed life that God in his grace is prepared to pour out on those who accept his Son as their Lord.

II. THE BLIND MEN BELIEVED THEY COULD EXPERIENCE GOD'S POWER IN THEIR LIVES.

A. These men asked for and fully expected God to perform a great work. Their faith gave God room to work in their lives.

B. In the same way, God led Gideon to expect a great blessing from him even when victory seemed impossible (Judges 6, 7). The widow of 2 Kings 4:1-7 was willing to give God all that she had, and she received back more than she ever needed.

III. THE BLIND MEN SEIZED THEIR ONE AND ONLY CHANCE TO MEET JESUS.

A. As far as we know, this is the only time Jesus ever went to Jericho. If these two blind men had not insisted on going to Jesus then, they would have missed the great blessing they received.

B. Many people are lost because, when they have the opportunity to meet Jesus and let him into their lives, they hesitate and are lost forever. We simply cannot wait to get right with God. We must seize the opportunity the moment it comes.

C. The philosophers on Mars Hill told Paul, "We want to hear you again on this subject" (Acts 17:32). To the best of our knowledge, they never did. Governor Felix said he wanted to hear the gospel some other time (Acts 24:24, 25). There is no record of his doing so.

D. General George C. Patton once said, "A good plan executed now is better than a perfect plan executed next week." If you need to be saved, if you need to have a closer walk with the Lord, if you need to deal with some sin in you life, you had better do it now!

IV. THE BLIND MEN REFUSED TO BE DISCOURAGED BY OTHERS.

A. The crowd demanded that these blind men keep silent, but they refused and insisted on coming to Jesus.

B. It is interesting that Luke introduces at least one of the blind men as Jesus approached the city (18:35), while Matthew describes the healing on the departure (20:29). It is possible these men failed to reach Jesus on his way into Jericho and had to make their way around the city to get to him.

C. Hebrews 11:6 says that anyone who comes to God must not only believe that he exists but "that he rewards those who earnestly seek him."

CONCLUSION

The blind men followed Jesus after he had healed them. These two men did not merely accept the relief of the moment. They readily gave themselves to the King. Considering all that Jesus has done for you, will you follow Jesus as well?

Who Are You Looking For?

John 20:1-18

Mary Magdalene was first among Jesus' female disciples, the leader of those who helped and cared for him and a special testimony to Christ's power to save and heal. She was also the first to witness the miracle of the resurrection.

We should look for Jesus first, boldly, faithfully, earnestly, and only.

I. MARY MAGDALENE LOOKED FOR JESUS FIRST.

A. Mary was the first person to see the empty tomb, the first person to meet Jesus after he rose from the dead, and the first person to tell the good news of his resurrection to someone else. Why? Because she was the first one at the tomb on Easter Sunday morning. Finding Jesus was her top priority.

B. Too many people put off coming to Christ until some later time. "I'll get around to it." "I'll do it when the time is right." Not Mary. She knew the time to look for Christ is right now.

II. MARY MAGDALENE LOOKED FOR JESUS BOLDLY.

A. Mary had dared to stand at the foot of Jesus' cross and later at his tomb. She was not afraid of the soldiers or the Jewish leaders and had no concern for her own safety or welfare. She was not ashamed of being identified with Jesus.

B. Mary's courage and boldness is remarkable especially in light of the fact that the disciples had fled when Jesus was arrested and were still hiding behind locked doors when Jesus appeared to them on Sunday evening (John 20:19). Even after Mary had rushed to tell Peter and John about the empty tomb and they had seen it for themselves, they "went back to their homes, but Mary stood outside the tomb" (John 20:10, 11).

C. It takes courage to follow Jesus, to be a Christian. There will be times when we must defy the world, when we must press on where others flee. If you would have Christ, seek him boldly. Let nothing hold you back.

III. MARY MAGDALENE LOOKED FOR JESUS FAITHFULLY.

A. Mary followed Christ throughout his ministry. As he was dying, she stood by him at the cross (John 19:25), and when he was dead, she stood by him at his grave. When at last Mary saw Jesus alive, she wanted to hold on to him with all her might (John 20:17).

B. We ought to seek Jesus that way, cleaving to the very least thing that has anything to do with him, remaining faithful even when all others might forsake him.

IV. MARY MAGDALENE LOOKED FOR JESUS EARNESTLY.

A. Mary was devastated at the suffering and death of the one she had loved so dearly. Her desire to find Jesus was deep, for Jesus meant more to her than anyone or anything else. That is why she "stood outside the tomb crying" (John 20:11).

B. You cannot microwave a relationship with the living God. Unless you make a deliberate, conscious effort to earnestly seek the deeper, eternal things of God, you will be consumed in a sea of triviality. It is only when you give God your prime time, not your spare time, that you can really know him and his plan for your life. If you want to find Jesus, weep after him. Seek him earnestly.

V. MARY MAGDALENE LOOKED FOR JESUS ONLY.

A. Mary not only saw two angels but also talked with them (John 20:12, 13). Although many would have focused on this supernatural encounter, she turned from the angels, searching only for Jesus (John 20:14).

B. If your heart is focused on Christ alone, if you have cast out all rivals, you will find him. Let us, like Mary, be satisfied with nothing short of Jesus.

CONCLUSION

Mary finally recognized Jesus when he called her name (John 20:16). Earlier Jesus had said that a good shepherd knows his sheep and calls them by name and that the sheep know their shepherd's voice (John 10:3, 4). Jesus also went on to call himself the "good shepherd" who loves and cares for us.

Can you hear Jesus' voice today? Is he calling your name? Will you look for and come to him as Mary did? Will you tell others the good news that he is risen?

The Man Who Was Late for Easter

John 20:24-31

History has not been kind to Thomas. Because of him, the term "Doubting Thomas" was introduced into our language. Thomas was not with the apostles that Sunday evening when Jesus first appeared to them, so when the other apostles told him they had seen the Lord, he didn't believe them. Even now Jesus invites us to ask and answer the question that was on Thomas's heart and lips that first Easter. Could it possibly be true? Did it really happen?

Jesus really was resurrected from the dead!

I. JESUS WAS ACTUALLY DEAD.

A. Some skeptics have concocted theories that Jesus fainted, rather than died, on the cross. But Jesus was seen to be *medically* dead (John 19:31-35) and was later pronounced *legally* dead by the Roman authorities (Mark 15:44, 45).

B. All four Gospels say that Jesus died on the cross. Ancient Roman, Jewish, and Greek historians agree that Jesus was executed (Tacitus, Josephus, Lucian). No one disputed that fact during the lifetime of the original witnesses.

II. JESUS WAS BURIED IN A SEALED, GUARDED TOMB.

A. The tomb was guarded and sealed to prevent removal of the body and to ensure that no false claim of a resurrection could be made. The Greek word *asphalizo*, "to make sure or secure," is used three times in Matthew 27:64-66. This word often describes the securing of a fortress or a military stronghold.

B. The tomb was secured by a large stone or boulder (Mark 16:4), a seal (Matthew 27:66), and a guard *(koustodia)* of Roman soldiers (Matthew 27:66), the fiercest, most well-disciplined soldiers in the ancient world.

III. THE TOMB WAS FOUND EMPTY ON EASTER MORNING.

A. All four Gospels report that the disciples found the tomb empty on Sunday morning. The Roman guards reported it empty. On Pentecost, when the apostles declared that Jesus had risen from the dead in the very city where he had been crucified and buried, no one even attempted to refute them. Everyone, including skeptics, admits that the tomb was empty.

B. Did the disciples steal the body?
1. The Roman guard had been posted for the very purpose of preventing such a theft (Matthew 27:62-64).
2. Stealing Jesus' body and then lying about the resurrection is foreign to the character of the disciples. On Thursday, they fled from the Garden of Gethsemane (Matthew 26:56; Mark 14:50-52), and when Jesus appeared to the disciples the evening he arose, they were hiding behind locked doors for fear of the Jews (John 20:19).
3. If the resurrection were a hoax, the disciples would not have put forth women as their chief witnesses because women were invalid witnesses according to Jewish principle of evidence.

IV. THE RISEN LORD WAS SEEN, HEARD, AND TOUCHED.

A. More than five hundred people saw Jesus alive over a period of forty days between his resurrection and ascension, and most of them were still living when Paul wrote to the Corinthians in A.D. 56 (l Corinthians 15:5-8).

B. Were the post-resurrection appearances hallucinations?
1. The appearances were witnessed by more than five hundred people on at least eleven separate occasions. Hallucinations are very individualistic. It is inconceivable that five hundred people in different groups, at different times, in different situations, should experience the same hallucination.
2. The disciples' belief that Jesus had appeared to them lasted well beyond the forty days they saw him. Belief in a hallucination usually ceases with the cessation of the hallucination, yet the apostles maintained their belief in Jesus' resurrection for the rest of their lives.
3. The disciples did not expect Jesus to rise from the dead. Hallucinations require a spirit of excited expectation to project something that really isn't there. The women came to anoint a dead body (Mark 16:1). When Mary first saw Jesus she mistook him for the gardener (John 20:14-16). The disciples dismissed the first report of the resurrection (Luke 24:11). Yet in the end they were convinced despite their own initial skepticism.
4. The disciples ate with Jesus. Hallucinations do not eat. They also do not serve breakfast. But the resurrected Jesus did, as recorded in Luke 24:30, 40-42; John 21:4-12; and Acts 10:39-41.

CONCLUSION

Like Thomas, we have every reason to believe that Jesus Christ conquered death and actually rose from the dead. And the only appropriate response we can make is to say to Christ, as Thomas did, "My Lord and my God!" (John 20:28). At the close of this story, the apostle John states that Jesus' miracles "are written that you may believe that Jesus is the Christ, the Son of God, and that by believing you may have life in his name" (John 20:30, 31). Are you ready, like Thomas, to confess Jesus as your Lord and God? Are you ready to believe in him and thus have life in his name?

On a Mission From God

Acts 9:1-22

Saul of Tarsus's miraculous encounter with Jesus on the Damascus road brought about one of the most remarkable transformations ever recorded in Scripture. So dramatic was the change in Saul's life that the Lord even changed his name. Saul the Pharisee became Paul the apostle. Saul's conversion to Christianity has such far-reaching implications for the history of the church that it is the only event recorded three times in the book of Acts.

**Our life-mission matters when we obey Jesus
instantly, completely, and persistently.**

I. THREE TRUTHS CHANGED SAUL'S LIFE FOREVER.
A. Jesus was alive.
 1. When Saul saw the bright light and heard the Lord call his name, he asked, "Who are you, Lord?" The reply could not have been a greater surprise: "I am Jesus, whom you are persecuting" (Acts 9:5).
 2. Jesus was no longer a dead carpenter from Nazareth who had recruited a few fishermen to stir up trouble. Saul stood face to face with the Son of God in all his glory!

B. Saul was a lost sinner who needed to be saved.
 1. When God sent Ananias to Saul, Ananias challenged Saul: "Get up, be baptized and wash your sins away, calling on his name" (Acts 22:16).
 2. Saul learned that not only had he been wrong about who Jesus was, he had been wrong about his own spiritual condition. He was a lost sinner who needed to be saved.

C. God had a life-mission for Saul.
 1. The church's greatest persecutor would become its greatest preacher.
 2. The "Hebrew of Hebrews" would become the apostle to the Gentiles (Philippians 3:5).
 3. The legalistic Pharisee would become the proclaimer of God's grace.

II. SAUL OBEYED JESUS INSTANTLY, COMPLETELY, AND PERSISTENTLY.

   A. Saul followed Jesus instantly.
   1. When Saul met Jesus on the Damascus road, he had only one question: "What shall I do, Lord?" (Acts 22:10). Instantly, in that single moment, Saul resigned from everything he had been and put himself under the authority of Jesus. Saul immediately obeyed the Lord.
   2. Likewise, now is the time to do whatever God has called you to do.

   B. Saul also followed Jesus completely. Jesus had all of Saul that there was to have (Philippians 3:12-14). Following Jesus is not something one can do halfheartedly.

   C. Saul followed Jesus persistently.
   1. For nearly twenty years, Paul traversed the Roman Empire, tirelessly proclaiming the good news about Jesus. No level of persecution could shut him up or distract him from his mission.
   2. When Paul stood on trial for his life, he recounted the day Jesus met him on the road to Damascus with these words: "So then, King Agrippa, I was not disobedient to the vision from heaven. First to those in Damascus, then to those in Jerusalem and in all Judea, and to the Gentiles also, I preached that they should repent and turn to God" (Acts 26:19, 20).

CONCLUSION

From the ashes of Saul's old life arose the noblest and most useful man of God the church has ever known. God not only transformed Saul's life but used him in the transformation of countless others.

Every believer should follow Saul's example in discovering and obeying God's call on his or her life. Not all of us are called to be preachers or missionaries, and not all of us will be called in a blinding light. But each of us was created to do something in God's service. Diligently seek God's call for your life, and when you discover what God wants you to do, obey him instantly, completely, and persistently.

ILLUSTRATION

Mel Trotter was a barber by trade, but his real aim in life was to drink himself into oblivion. Trotter says that for most of his adult life he was simply a common drunk. He became so depraved that when his little girl died, he stole the shoes she was to be buried in and pawned them for money to buy more drinks.

One night, however, Mel staggered into the Pacific Garden Mission in Chicago and found Christ. After becoming a Christian, Mel Trotter not only gave up alcohol but came to have a great passion for reaching men on skid row. So he opened a rescue mission in Grand Rapids, Michigan. In time he went on to found more than sixty more missions stretching from Boston to San Francisco. Mel Trotter is a remarkable testimony to the life-changing power of the gospel.

Making a Difference

Matthew 5:13-16

Salt has always been a valuable commodity. Since prehistoric times, it has been universally used as a seasoning and a preservative. Salt is so valuable that it has sometimes been used as money. So Jesus could not have used a more vivid word picture to describe how important his followers' influence would be in the world.

God calls us to be different so that we can make a difference.

I. GOD PUT US IN THE WORLD TO MAKE A DIFFERENCE.

A. When Jesus speaks about our being the salt of the earth and the light of the world, he's talking about our *influence*. Consciously or unconsciously, our character affects everyone who knows us.

B. The classic film, *It's a Wonderful Life,* tells the story of George Bailey, who thinks that his life counts for nothing because he has never been able to get out of the small town of Bedford Falls, where he is the president of the local Building and Loan Association. When Christmas Eve 1945 finds George with more problems than he thinks he can handle, he tries to end his life by jumping off a bridge. He is saved, however, by his guardian angel, Clarence, who shows George what his town would have been like if it hadn't been for all his good deeds. When George sees how much worse Bedford Falls would have been without his influence, Clarence tells George, "One man's life touches so many others that when he's not there it leaves an awfully big hole."

C. No one can enter this world without increasing or diminishing the sum total of goodness and righteousness. You cannot detach yourself from this connection. You cannot withdraw your moral influence on the universe. By the time your life is done, there will be thousands of people who will enter eternity with a different character than they would have if you had never lived. You leave your fingerprints on the soul of every person you meet.

D. The pronoun "you" is emphatic in Matthew 5:13 and 14. Jesus is saying, "You are the [only] salt of the earth. . . . You are the [only] light of the world." The corruption and darkness of the world will not be penetrated unless Christians do it. Our influence flows from who and what we are.

II. WE INFLUENCE OTHERS BY OUR WALK AND BY OUR WITNESS.

A. When Jesus said that we are salt, he was speaking of the influence of our Christian *walk*—the way we live.

1. Salt is not only a seasoning but also a preservative. In the ancient world, before refrigeration, meat would rot unless it was salted. Christians are in the world to preserve it, to retard its moral spoilage and corruption.

2. Edmund Burke said, "The only thing necessary for the triumph of evil is for good men to do nothing." In business, politics, education, and society in general, someone has to draw the line. That is our job.

3. Most people in the world do not have the moral courage to take a stand by themselves, but many of them will follow if someone gives them a lead. That is our job—to give them that lead.

B. When Jesus said that we are light, he was speaking of the influence of our Christian *witness*—what we say to lead others to him. Light is a guide. We need it to find our way in dark places. All of us know people who will not find their way to Christ unless we tell them how.

III. WE MUST BE DIFFERENT IN ORDER TO MAKE A DIFFERENCE.

A. In Matthew 5:13, Jesus says that if the salt loses its saltiness, "It is no longer good for anything, except to be thrown out and trampled by men."

1. Contaminated salt is useless. In Jesus' day, it was thrown away. But one had to be careful not to throw it on a garden or field, where it would kill vegetation. So it was thrown onto a path or roadway, where it would be ground into the dirt and disappear.

2. When we become contaminated by sin, we lose our usefulness as God's moral preservative in the world. We cannot be an influence for purity unless we are pure.

B. In verse 15 Jesus says that it doesn't do any good to light a lamp and then hide it under a bowl. Christianity is something that is meant to be seen. Jesus did not say, "You are the light of the *church*," but "You are the light of the *world*." We must reach out to the people in darkness in order to give them light.

CONCLUSION

In the Garden of Gethsemane, Jesus offered this prayer for his followers:

> My prayer is not that you take them out of the world but that you protect them from the evil one. They are not of the world, even as I am not of it. . . . As you sent me into the world, I have sent them into the world (John 17:15, 16, 18).

That is our challenge: to be *in* the world but not *of* the world. God put us here to make a difference.

Putting an End to Worry

Matthew 6:25-33

Worry is the sin of distrusting the promise and providence of God, yet it is a sin that Christians commit perhaps more frequently than any other. The heart of Jesus' message in our present passage is . . .

Don't worry—not even about life's necessities.

I. DON'T WORRY BECAUSE YOU ARE A SERVANT OF GOD, AND YOUR WELFARE IS HIS BUSINESS, NOT YOURS.

A. Matthew 6:25 says, "Therefore I tell you, do not worry about your life, what you will eat or drink; or about your body, what you will wear. Is not life more important than food, and the body more important than clothes?"

B. Note that verse 25 begins with the word "therefore." In the previous verse, Jesus had said, "No one can serve two masters. Either he will hate the one and love the other, or he will be devoted to the one and despise the other. You cannot serve both God and Money." As Christians, God is our master. In biblical times, the master of a house had complete responsibility for the welfare of his servants, so our care is completely in God's hands.

C. Unbelievers, however, are on their own. Matthew 6:31, 32 explains, "So do not worry, saying, 'What shall we eat?' or 'What shall we drink?' or 'What shall we wear?' *For the pagans run after all these things,* and your heavenly Father knows that you need them."

II. DON'T WORRY BECAUSE YOUR MASTER OWNS EVERYTHING.

A. Psalm 24:1 teaches us, "The earth is the Lord's, and everything in it, the world, and all who live in it." Everything we now have belongs to the Lord. Everything we will ever have actually belongs to the Lord.

B. Instead of focusing on what you may or may not have, you should trust in the promise that "God will meet all your needs according to his glorious riches in Christ Jesus" (Philippians 4:19).

III. DON'T WORRY BECAUSE YOUR MASTER IS IN CONTROL OF EVERYTHING.

A. In 1 Chronicles 29:12, David praises God as follows: "You are the ruler of all things. In your hands are strength and power to exalt and give strength to all."

B. Daniel's recognition of God's total control leads him to exclaim, "Praise be to the name of God for ever and ever; wisdom and power are his. He changes times and seasons; he sets up kings and deposes them" (Daniel 2:20, 21).

IV. DON'T WORRY BECAUSE YOUR MASTER WILL PROVIDE EVERYTHING YOU WILL EVER NEED.

A. There is no reason to worry about food, for Matthew 6:26 states, "Look at the birds of the air; they do not sow or reap or store away in barns, and yet your heavenly Father feeds them. Are you not much more valuable than they?"

B. There is no reason to worry about longevity, as Matthew 6:27 reminds us, "Who of you by worrying can add a single hour to his life?"

C. Finally, there is no reason to worry about one's clothing. Matthew 6:28-30 says,
> And why do you worry about clothes? See how the lilies of the field grow. They do not labor or spin. Yet I tell you that not even Solomon in all his splendor was dressed like one of these. If that is how God clothes the grass of the field, which is here today and tomorrow is thrown into the fire, will he not much more clothe you, O you of little faith?"

V. DON'T WORRY BECAUSE YOUR MASTER HAS YOUR ETERNAL DESTINY IN HIS HANDS.

A. God not only takes care of our material needs but has prepared something far better for us: "But seek first his kingdom and his righteousness, and all these things will be given to you as well" (6:33)

B. The unbeliever has nothing except the perishable things of this world, but we possess eternal life and an eternal legacy.

CONCLUSION

Worry is the opposite of contentment, which should be the normal and consistent state of mind of every believer. Worry is not a trivial sin. To worry is to distrust God and his Word. All of us should be able to say with the apostle Paul:
> I have learned to be content whatever the circumstances. I know what it is to be in need, and I know what it is to have plenty. I have learned the secret of being content in any and every situation, whether well fed or hungry, whether living in plenty or in want. I can do everything through him who gives me strength (Philippians 4:11-13).

Let God Sort 'Em Out

Matthew 13:24-30, 36-43

The Bible speaks of a future, but certain, judgment, a time when God will divide those who have accepted him from those who rejected him. The former will enjoy eternal bliss in God's presence, while the latter will suffer unending punishment. Until that day of final reckoning, however, God is in the business of making wheat out of weeds, saints out of sinners.

Like God, we should be in the business of making wheat out of weeds.

I. JUDGMENT DAY IS COMING.

A. Jesus teaches that there will come a day when the wheat (the church) will be gathered into God's barn (Heaven), while the weeds (the world) will be thrown into the fire (Hell).

B. Hell exists for several reasons.
  1. Justice demands it. Not all evil is punished in this life, as Psalm 73:1-20 explains.
  2. God's sovereignty demands it. If there is no ultimate separation of good from evil, no final victory of good over evil, then God really is not in control.
  3. Human dignity demands it. Part of our being created "in God's image" (Genesis 1:26, 27) is our free will, the power to make unconstrained, voluntary, and therefore responsible choices. We have the freedom to refuse God's love.

C. Acts 17:31 says that God "has set a day when he will judge the world with justice." Revelation 20:11-15 describes that day of judgment. Therefore, we can be certain that Judgment Day is coming.

II. THE CHURCH AGE IS FOR EVANGELISM, NOT JUDGMENT.

A. Although there will be a time for judgment, this is not it. The parable of the wheat and weeds says that God will permit the church and the wicked people of this world to live side by side until the Judgment Day.

B. Matthew 13:28-30 explains why: "The servants asked him, 'Do you want us to go and pull them up?' 'No,' he answered, 'because while you are pulling the weeds, you may root up the wheat with them. Let both grow together until the harvest.'"

C. The church is called to preach and teach against sin. However, our purpose for doing that is not to judge people but to win them to Christ.
  1. God has called us to witness, not to condemn. Our job is not to convict but to convert sinners, not to pass sentence but to share the gospel.
  2. Besides, none of us is qualified to infallibly determine who is saved and who is not.

III. WE MUST BE SURE THAT WE ARE WHEAT AND NOT A WEED.

A. Jesus closed his explanation of this parable with these words: "He who has ears, let him hear" (Matthew 13:43). In addition to calling us to reach lost people with the gospel, the parable also reminds each of us to seriously face the question of whether we are wheat or a weed.

B. Too often people attempt to avoid their responsibility to obey the gospel by pointing to someone else. None of us is in a position to say how God will deal with someone else's soul. We can only act on the gospel ourselves as we encourage others to do the same.

CONCLUSION

In Luke 15:10, Jesus said, "There is rejoicing in the presence of the angels of God over one sinner who repents." Let us be sure that we obey the gospel, then let us extend God's love and mercy to everyone we can while there is time. Let us make evangelism the centerpiece of every program and ministry of our church and the personal responsibility and passion of every member.

ILLUSTRATION

In 1992, a Los Angeles parking control officer happened upon a brown Cadillac El Dorado illegally parked next to the curb on street-sweeping day. The officer dutifully wrote out a ticket. Ignoring the man seated behind the wheel of the car, he reached in and placed the $30 ticket on the dashboard.

The man in the car made no excuses. He didn't argue or try to stop the officer, and for good reason. The driver was dead. He had been shot in the head ten to twelve hours earlier but was sitting up, stiff as a board, slumped slightly forward with blood on his face.

The officer, preoccupied with ticket-writing, later said he was unaware of anything out of the ordinary. He simply got back in his car and drove off to the next illegally parked car.

As grisly as that story is, it points to a very important truth for us in the church. Many people around us are dead in their sins. What should catch our attention is their need, not their offenses. What they need most is not our citations nor our judgments. What they need most is our Savior.

What's the Kingdom Worth?

Matthew 13:44-46

Everyone enjoys a story of treasure found. It appeals to our secret desires to be wealthy and secure. But Jesus told the story of two men who found treasure for a different reason, to teach us what his kingdom is actually worth.

**The kingdom of God costs everything we have
but is worth far more than anything it costs.**

I. ENTERING GOD'S KINGDOM COSTS EVERYTHING WE HAVE.

A. Both the man who found the treasure and the man who found the pearl sold everything they had in order to obtain the prize they sought.

B. In the same way, being a Christian demands nothing less than willingly sacrificing everything for the sake of following Christ (Matthew 10:37-39; Romans 12:1).

II. GOD'S KINGDOM IS WORTH INFINITELY MORE THAN WHAT IT COSTS.

A. The man who bought the field found "a treasure" (Matthew 13:44). The Greek word used here, *thesauros*, refers to a treasure chest or storehouse where a great treasure is kept. It is the same word used in Hebrews 11:26 to describe Moses' turning of his back on the "treasures of Egypt" in order to follow God.

B. The pearl merchant found a pearl "of great value." The Greek word used to describe the pearl, *polutimos*, means something that is very expensive, of great worth, or priceless. It is the word used of the expensive perfume with which Jesus was anointed before his crucifixion (John 12:3). In 1 Peter 1:7, Peter describes our faith as being "of greater worth *[polutimos]* than gold."

C. Belonging to God's kingdom, being God's child, is a priceless experience. Nothing else on earth can wash the dark stains of sin from our lives, can purify the foulest sinful heart, can give real peace to a troubled mind, can calm life's roughest storms, can cheer our darkest hours, can give faith and courage that defy even death, or can secure the blessing of eternal life.

D. Finally, verse 44 says that the man who found the treasure in the field "*in his joy* went and sold all he had and bought that field." Being part of God's kingdom will bring you greater joy than you can possibly imagine.

III. YOU MUST CHOOSE TO BELONG TO GOD'S KINGDOM.

A. In each parable, a man made the decision to sacrifice everything he had in order to gain something that had become immeasurably valuable to him. In the same way, we cannot inherit salvation. We must make a personal choice to join God's kingdom. Being born into a Christian family, having Christian friends, or even attending a Christian church does not make you a Christian. You must make your own personal decision to commit your life to Christ.

B. Some people find God as the man found the treasure in a field. They aren't looking for God, but in the ordinary course of their lives God finds them. Some people find God like the merchant who spent his life looking for the pearl of great price. They are looking for God, searching for truth, hungry for meaning, purpose, and direction for their lives, and at last they find him. However you come to discover the kingdom of God, there comes a point at which you must make a personal decision to enter it by entrusting your life to Christ.

CONCLUSION

Belonging to God's kingdom is a priceless treasure that exceeds all earthly riches and advantages combined. God offers this priceless treasure to anyone—no matter how poor, how insignificant, or how sinful—who accepts Christ.

How Many Times Shall I Forgive?

Matthew 18:21-35

Alexander Pope once noted, "To err is human, to forgive divine." There is nothing that so perfectly characterizes God as forgiveness—and nothing makes us more like him than to forgive. But are there limits to forgiveness? Jesus answers with a simple parable.

We can forgive others without limit because God has done the same for us.

I. REAL FORGIVENESS HAS NO LIMITS.

    A. The parable begins with a simple question: "Peter came to Jesus and asked, 'Lord, how many times shall I forgive my brother when he sins against me? Up to seven times?'" (Matthew 18:21).

        1. Peter understood human nature well enough to know that all of us are "repeat offenders" who need forgiveness. Peter simply wanted to know what the limit on forgiveness should be.

        2. The limit that Peter suggested, up to seven times, was more than twice that required by Jewish tradition and probably seemed generous to him.

    B. So Jesus' answer probably came as somewhat of a surprise (Matthew 18:22). Jesus took Peter's number, multiplied it by itself, and then by ten, to reach a number that no one would bother counting to.

        1. Jesus wasn't extending the limits of forgiveness. He was removing them.

        2. A Christian with a forgiving heart doesn't keep records but forgives the one hundredth offense as readily as the first.

    C. On yet another occasion, Jesus taught that even if a brother "sins against you seven times in a day, and seven times comes back to you and says, 'I repent,' forgive him" (Luke 17:4).

    D. This is what God does, for Romans 5:20 states that "where sin increased, grace increased all the more." Likewise, we should never allow a fellow believer's sin to surpass our willingness to forgive.

II. WE FORGIVE OTHERS BECAUSE GOD HAS FORGIVEN US.

    A. Jesus follows up his answer to Peter with a parable of two servants who owed debts that they could not pay. The king forgave the debt of the first servant who owed a sum equal to about two hundred thousand years' wages. But that man promptly forgot the grace and forgiveness he had received and refused to forgive his fellow servant a debt of only several months' wages. Understandably, the king was angry with the first servant because he had been forgiven all and should have forgiven all in turn.

B. The moral of the story is that Christians have a divine obligation to forgive those who wrong us. We never have grounds to withhold forgiveness. In addition, since God requires us to forgive, he must have made it possible for us to do so. What steps, then, should we take to develop the forgiving hearts that God requires?

APPLICATION

In his excellent book, *Forgive and Forget: Healing the Hurts We Don't Deserve*, Lewis Smedes says that there are four stages of forgiving. Understanding these four stages can help us practice forgiveness.

1. **We hurt.** The kinds of hurts that require forgiveness are usually personal, unfair, and deep. Forgiveness does not mean acting as though you weren't hurt. Real forgiveness begins by acknowledging the hurt.

2. **We hate.** Hate is a natural human response to any deep and unfair pain. At times it is a passive hate that simply robs you of the energy to wish a person well. Sometimes it is an aggressive hate that wishes them ill. Whether it is passive or aggressive, hate separates us from people we should belong to.

3. **We heal ourselves.** The first step in healing a hurt takes place within your own heart. When you forgive someone, you perform spiritual surgery on your own soul. *You* choose to let go of *your* bitterness and hate and rewrite the history between you and the person who wronged you.

4. **We come together.** The goal of forgiveness is to invite the person who hurt and wronged you back into your life. You extend your hand to that person and invite him or her to cross over the wall that wrong and hate have built between you. Realistically, it isn't always possible to restore a relationship to exactly what it was before. But when we forgive, we start over on whatever terms that time and circumstances make available to us.

ILLUSTRATION

A traveler through Burma forded a river. When he emerged on the other side, he found his body covered with small blood-sucking leeches. His first impulse was to pull them off, but his guide warned against it, explaining that to do so would leave part of the leeches buried in the skin and cause serious infection. Instead, the native prepared a warm bath for the man and added to the water certain herbs that caused the leeches to voluntarily drop off.

Unforgiven injuries are like leeches draining us of spiritual life. Yet the mere human determination to cast them off often leaves emotional poison in our souls. Only bathing ourselves in God's mercy and love—constantly reminding ourselves of how much we have been forgiven—will empower us to forgive those who sin against us.

Ready or Not, Here He Comes

Matthew 25:1-13

When Jesus ascended into Heaven, he promised that he would return to judge the world, cast the devil and his followers into Hell, and take the church to live forever with him in Heaven. The Bible warns us to be ready for the second coming of Christ.

Because we don't know when Jesus will return, we should keep ourselves ready at all times.

I. SOME THINGS CANNOT BE PUT OFF UNTIL THE LAST MINUTE.

A. The bridesmaids were supposed to have their lamps ready to light the way for the wedding party to go on to the wedding feast. But when the groom arrived, only five bridesmaids were ready. The other five had waited too long. The shops were all closed. It was too late to go and buy oil.

B. Procrastination is a bad habit at all times. But it will be a fatal mistake for those not ready to meet Christ when he returns. Jesus is teaching the importance of being prepared to meet him when he returns, because after he appears, unbelievers will have no further chance for salvation.

C. Years ago C. S. Lewis wrote, "When Christ returns, how awful to know that all of it was true, and that it is too late to do anything about it."

II. SOME THINGS JUST CAN'T BE BORROWED.

A. The foolish virgins could not borrow oil when they needed it. In the same way, people cannot borrow a personal relationship with God. They must possess it for themselves. They cannot live on someone else's spiritual capital.

B. For example, it is the practice of some churches to christen babies. In most christening ceremonies the child's godparents answer questions and make promises on the child's behalf. On the basis of these answers and promises, the child is sprinkled with water and is said to have been "baptized" into the Christian faith. However, biblical baptism is always preceded by faith. As Jesus stated in Mark 16:16, "Whoever believes and is baptized will be saved." In the New Testament, only believers are baptized.

C. No one else can answer for you. You must make a personal commitment to Christ to become a Christian. And when Christ returns, what others have said or done for you will not matter—only what you have decided for Christ.

III. SOME THINGS SIMPLY DO NOT NEED TO BE KNOWN.

A. Jesus stated the point of this parable as follows: "Therefore keep watch, because you do not know the day or the hour" (Matthew 25:13). Some people become so caught up in trying to figure out elaborately detailed scenarios of the second coming and match the biblical prophecies with contemporary events that the real message of Christ's return gets lost.

B. The second coming, however, is an event that is beyond our power to imagine. It is enough to take the plain, simple truth of Scripture that
1. Jesus will return to earth visibly and victoriously.
2. His return will bring about the end of time and the beginning of eternity.
3. When Jesus comes back, he will judge the world, send the devil and his followers to Hell, and take his church to live with him forever in Heaven.

C. There is little value in going beyond those basic facts that are clearly and repeatedly taught in Scripture. It is enough to recognize that the Lord is coming back, that we don't know when, and that we need to live our lives in a state of readiness for his return.

D. The return of Christ will have the same significance for Christians alive when it happens as death has for Christians who die before it happens: it will be the end of life in this world and the start of life in what has been described as "an unknown environment with a well-known inhabitant."

IV. SOME THINGS SIMPLY MUST NOT BE MISSED.

A. The foolish virgins missed the joy of the wedding feast because they were not ready when the groom came. Let us make sure that we do not miss the indescribably greater joy that will come to those who attend Jesus' wedding feast.

B. The New Testament uses a beautiful Greek term to describe Jesus' return: *parousia* (1 Thessalonians 4:15-18). In ancient times the term referred to a visit of a person of high rank, especially the king or the emperor. Knowing that the King of kings will return to this earth, let us follow the example of Martin Luther, who said he had only two days on his calendar, today and "that day."

CONCLUSION

Jesus said, "Therefore keep watch, because you do not know the day or the hour" (Matthew 25:13). Becoming a Christian is not something to put off. Serving Christ faithfully is not something to neglect. When Jesus comes, may he find us ready.

Are You a Responsible Servant?

Matthew 25:14-30

God has given every believer certain gifts and abilities. Some are enabled to teach, while others are empowered to show mercy. Unfortunately, sometimes Christians focus so much on the gifts they do not have that they forget to use the ones they do have. Jesus warns us against such an attitude in the parable of the talents.

Each of us is responsible to use the gifts God gave us to accomplish his work.

I. BOTH THE SERVANTS AND THE TALENTS BELONGED TO THE MASTER.

A. The fact that the master in the story owned both the slaves and the talents he gave to them reflects a basic biblical principle: God owns everything, "the world, and all who live in it" (Psalm 24:1).

B. This morning you woke up to another one of God's days in God's world. The house you slept in was made of wood from God's trees or brick from the elements of God's earth. The food you ate for breakfast came from God's fields and farms. The next breath you take will be a breath of God's air. But, you may say, I own that house. I paid for that food. Who gave you the abilities that you use to earn an income? Who gave you the mind and the body that you use to work? Feel your pulse. Do you have any control over whether or not your heart takes its next beat? Your very life belongs to God.

C. To become a Christian is to become a servant or slave of Christ. According to 1 Corinthians 6:19, 20, "You are not your own; you were bought at a price. Therefore honor God with your body."

II. THE MASTER ENTRUSTED EACH SERVANT WITH SOMETHING OF GREAT VALUE.

A. In biblical times, a denarius equaled one day's wage for a laborer. A talent was worth about six thousand denarii. So the amount entrusted even to the least servant was equal to nearly twenty years' wages!

B. Whatever gifts, abilities, time, money, influence, or opportunities God has given you are incredibly valuable.

C. Jesus was in the temple on another occasion, observing the people who came into the temple treasury to give their offerings (Luke 21:1-4). The treasury contained thirteen trumpet-shaped receptacles into which people would put their gifts. Jesus watched the rich put in their gifts, then a poor widow who put in two mites (Greek: *lepta*), the smallest denomination of Jewish money. Her gift was worth about half a cent. But the Lord knew it was all she had. The traditional law of that time said that no one was permitted to put in less than two *lepta*. She had that. She had just enough to do the smallest thing that was permitted. Without compromise, without hesitation, she devoted everything she had to God. The Lord noticed, and he's still watching today.

III. THE AMOUNT ENTRUSTED TO EACH SERVANT WAS IN KEEPING WITH HIS ABILITY.

A. Matthew 25:15 says, "To one he gave five talents of money, to another two talents, and to another one talent, each according to his ability."

B. People vary greatly in their natural talents, intellect, wealth, opportunities, and other resources. In the church, people differ in their spiritual gifts and levels of responsibility. But we all have a common accountability to use whatever the Lord has entrusted to us on his behalf until he returns.

IV. THE MASTER EXPECTED AND REWARDED FRUITFUL OBEDIENCE.

A. The servants who wisely used what the master entrusted to them received a great reward. They were commended as "good and faithful" servants, given even greater things to do, and invited to share their master's happiness.

B. The faithless servant was condemned for wasting his opportunity. He was not punished because he failed. He was punished for not even trying, for doing nothing with what the master had given him. He made the mistake of thinking that the safest response was no response.

C. The principle taught by this parable is "Use it or lose it." The Christian life is a task, a mission, and an adventure. It is not for the timid, the lazy, or the faithless. God owns 100 percent of the shares of your life. He expects a return on his investment.

APPLICATION

Though the master was gone a long time, he did return to settle accounts with his servants. When Jesus returns, he will want to know what you have done with the life he gave you.

Though we are not saved by our works, there's no such thing as a saving faith that is not also a serving faith. Church isn't something you watch. It's something you do. What are you doing for him? Are you doing the best with what you have? What kind of fruit will you be able to show the Master when he returns?

The Power to Change Lives

Luke 5:36-39

In biblical times, wine was put into leather bottles called wineskins. Because new wine expands as it ferments, it was usually put in a new wineskin, which was soft and pliable and could expand with the wine. Over time a wineskin would dry out and become hard. If you put new wine into an old wineskin, you would ruin the wineskin and lose the wine.

The same is true of using a new piece of cloth to repair a hole in an old garment. Because the new cloth shrinks when it is washed and because it is stronger than the old cloth, it will tear an even larger hole in the old garment. Jesus used these two analogies to teach us an important lesson about the gospel.

**The gospel is a radical, life-changing power
that demands certain changes from us.**

I. THE GOSPEL WILL CHANGE YOUR LIFE FOREVER.

A. In John 3:3, Jesus said, "I tell you the truth, no one can see the kingdom of God unless he is born again." In 2 Corinthians 5:17, the apostle Paul stated the same principle in different words: "if anyone is in Christ, he is a new creation; the old has gone, the new has come!"

B. Becoming a Christian is the most dramatic change you could ever undergo: a supernatural renovation of your fallen human nature. When you become a Christian, you begin a lifelong process that will transform you down to the very core of your being. Be prepared to be stretched, for that is exactly what the "new wine" of the gospel will do to you when Christ comes into your life.

II. THE GOSPEL WILL CHANGE YOUR BELIEFS.

A. The Jewish leaders of Jesus' day found it difficult to accept his teaching because their minds were hardened by centuries of ritual and tradition. They had so encumbered God's Word with their own opinions that they could not see the truth when he was standing before their very eyes. As a result, Jesus condemned them for "setting aside the commands of God in order to observe your own traditions!" (Mark 7:9).

B. As a church, what we believe and what we practice must be governed by this principle: "In essentials, unity. In opinions, liberty. And in all things love."

1. An essential is any belief or behavior for which we have a clear New Testament commandment or example. Such things are binding on all Christians. Everything else is a matter of opinion or expediency, and we must be flexible on these matters.
2. Our aim is to speak where the Bible speaks and be silent where the Bible is silent.

C. Through the ages people have done to the New Testament exactly what the Pharisees did to the Old. They have encumbered the clear, simple teaching of God's Word with human creeds and traditions. The Bible alone is our authority, and we must constantly guard against approaching God's Word with our own preconceived ideas and theological baggage.

III. THE GOSPEL WILL CHANGE YOUR CHURCH.

A. When a church shares the good news about Jesus, people will accept Christ and the church will grow. Change is inescapable when growth takes place.

B. The very first church in Jerusalem experienced the change of rapid growth, expanding from 120 to 3,000 to over 5,000 members in just a few months. The first Jewish Christians also had to face a radical change of thinking when Gentiles began to accept Christ and became part of the church.

C. Change is not only an effect of growth, however, it is also a prerequisite for it. New methods, new tools, new ways of organizing and ministering are constantly needed if the church is to effectively reach each new generation for Christ. Our job is to take a gospel that never changes to a world that will never stay the same.

APPLICATION

Jesus recognized that all of us are naturally resistant to change. In Luke 5:39, Jesus concludes the parable of the wineskins with these words: "No one after drinking old wine wants the new, for he says, 'The old is better.'"

As we are faithful to the gospel, God's Word will continue to change us. And as our church is faithful to the Great Commission by winning people to Christ, we will continue to undergo change. To do that gracefully we must be flexible, patient, and positive. May God continually renew and refresh us so that we are always ready for the new blessings he will send us through the life-changing power of the gospel.

ILLUSTRATION

Hebrews 11:21 states: "By faith Jacob, when he was dying, blessed each of Joseph's sons, and worshiped as he leaned on the top of his staff." Jacob's entire life had been a great adventure of faith that had carried him to the promised land. And now in the evening of his years he still had his traveling staff in his hand, still ready for the open road. He was still ready to go wherever God wanted to take him. If we are to fully embrace the challenge of changing faith, we must never lose our spirit of adventure.

How Is Your Heart Soil?

Luke 8:4-15

As Jesus told the story of the sower, it is quite possible his listeners looked out into the fields and saw a man actually sowing seed. It was a familiar scene in Palestine. In contrast to the way we plant seed, Palestinian farmers in Jesus' day usually plowed their fields after sowing their seed. The grain was scattered on the ground from an open basket, which was replenished from a large sack of seed tied to the back of a donkey. The seed was then plowed into the ground for protection and germination.

When Jesus explained the parable to his disciples, we learn that he was trying to teach them (and us) what will happen when we share the gospel with other people. The seed represents the word of God. When we share the gospel with others, we are sowing the seed of God's Word into their lives. We refer to this story as the parable of the sower, but we ought to call it the parable of the soils, for the focus of the story is the four kinds of soil that represent four kinds of hearts we will encounter when we share the gospel.

Only those who produce fruit have truly implanted God's Word in their lives.

I. THE RESISTANT HEARER NEVER ACCEPTS THE TRUTH.

A. When broadcasting seed by hand, it was impossible to accurately control where all the seeds fell. Some seeds would fall onto the hard, untilled ground along the narrow paths separating one field from another (Luke 8:5, 12). These seeds would either be eaten by birds, who often followed farmers as they sowed their fields, or trampled under foot by travelers as they walked along the paths. Either way, these seeds never even sprouted.

B. The hard-packed soil along the path represents the people who hear the gospel but harden their hearts against it. Jesus said that when we harden our hearts, we make it easy for the devil to come and snatch away the seed of God's Word. Each time someone resists the gospel, it becomes easier to resist it the next time.

II. THE SHALLOW HEARER FALLS AWAY FROM THE TRUTH.

A. Some soil in Palestine covers unseen layers of rock that prevent the plants from growing deep roots. The seeds that fell on such ground would spring up immediately, but as the plant developed, its roots could not penetrate the rock just below the surface (Luke 8:13). These little plants would often appear healthier than those in good soil, because more of them showed above ground and they grew faster. But after a while the sun would scorch them because they lacked good roots. They would quickly wither away.

B. This soil represents superficial converts. Jesus explained that when shallow converts face a time of testing, when things get tough, when they have to take a stand for their faith in the face of opposition, they fall away. While the superficial hearer falls away *immediately* after trouble or persecution comes, it could be *several years* before this person is tested by such trials.

C. We must be careful that we do not encourage a shallow acceptance of the gospel by engaging in a shallow evangelism. We must not hold out the blessings of salvation while hiding its costs.

III. THE DISTRACTED HEARER FORGETS ABOUT THE TRUTH.

A. A third type of ground where the seeds fell was infested with thorns (Luke 8:14). The soil might appear fertile after it had been cultivated, but when the grain began to sprout, so did the thorns. These tough, thistle-bearing weeds would choke out the good plants by taking up most of the space, moisture, and nutrients in the soil.

B. Food, shelter, clothing, and human companionship are all necessities of life. But when our physical passions and possessions become the focus of our lives, they become weeds and thorns that choke out the influence of God's Word. Thus 1 John 2:15, 16 warns us against loving the world or anything in it.

IV. THE RECEPTIVE HEARER MULTIPLIES THE TRUTH.

A. Most of the seed would fall into the good soil. It was away from the path and was loose and soft. It had sufficient depth to support the good plants and was free of weeds. The Lord said that when his seed fell into that kind of good soil, it would produce an abundant crop.

B. The difference between the good soil and the others is not its composition, but its condition. Anyone willing to accept Jesus Christ on God's terms is good soil. Just as you can tell good soil by the crop it bears, so the ultimate mark of the genuine believer is the spiritual fruit in that person's life (see Galatians 5:22, 23).

CONCLUSION

Jesus' teaching here should encourage all of us to share the gospel with everyone we know. Despite the fact that some of the people to whom we witness will be hard, shallow, or worldly, there are always those whose hearts are good soil. The parable should also remind each of us to keep our hearts broken and soft so God's Word will continually find root in us and his good fruit will grow in our lives.

Who Is My Neighbor?

Luke 10:25-37

People ask questions for different reasons. Some questions are genuine requests for information, while others are intended to make a point. Still other questions seek to change the subject and thereby avoid some sort of unpleasantness. Such was the case with the lawyer in this parable. He asked Jesus, "Who is my neighbor," but the real question is, "Am I a good neighbor?"

Good neighbors show active compassion even when it costs them to do so.

I. BEING A GOOD NEIGHBOR STARTS WITH COMPASSION.

A. The story of the good Samaritan flows out of the discussion of what were the greatest commandments. Jesus said they were to love God and to love one's neighbor.

B. Luke 10:33 says that when the Samaritan saw the wounded man he "took pity on" or had compassion for him. The Greek word used in this verse *(splanchnizomai)* literally means "to be moved in the inward parts." It describes someone deeply moved with compassion. It is frequently used to describe Jesus' compassion toward people in need (Mark 1:40-42; Luke 15:20).

C. In John 13:34, 35, Jesus says, "A new command I give you: Love one another. As I have loved you, so you must love one another. By this all men will know that you are my disciples, if you love one another." The principal characteristic that marks us as followers of Jesus Christ is that we *love* one another.

II. A GOOD NEIGHBOR PUTS COMPASSION INTO ACTION.

A. The dangerous condition of the road from Jerusalem to Jericho reveals that it is far easier to maintain a religious system than it is to clean up a neighborhood.

B. Many of the biblical commandments deal with our responsibilities toward our neighbors. For example, the last of the Ten Commandments is, "You shall not covet your neighbor's house [or] wife, or his manservant or maidservant, his ox or donkey, or anything that belongs to your neighbor" (Exodus 20:17).

C. Yet these responsibilities must be met from an attitude of compassion. Romans 13:8-10 commands:

> Let no debt remain outstanding, except the continuing debt to love one another, for he who loves his fellowman has fulfilled the law. The commandments . . . are summed up in this one rule: "Love your neighbor as yourself." Love does no harm to its neighbor. Therefore love is the fulfillment of the law.

D. The Bible defines love in terms of things we do and don't do. Note that Jesus ended the story of the Good Samaritan by saying, "Go and do likewise." He did not tell the lawyer, "Go and *feel* likewise," but "Go and *do* likewise."

III. A GOOD NEIGHBOR CARES EVEN THOUGH IT COSTS.

A. Luke 10:34, 35 says the Samaritan: 1) went to the wounded man, 2) poured oil and wine onto his wounds, 3) bandaged him, 4) put the man on his own donkey, 5) took him to an inn and cared for him through the night, 6) gave the innkeeper two day's wages to continue looking after the man until he got well, and 7) made arrangements to reimburse the innkeeper if the wounded man needed anything extra.

B. Love costs. The Samaritan demonstrated that the care we show to others should be measured by the care we would show to ourselves.

APPLICATION

So, who is our neighbor? The lawyer asked Jesus the question hoping to limit his responsibility to love and care for other people. But Jesus changed the question to "Am I a neighbor to those around me?"

To the thieves, the traveling Jew was a victim to exploit. To the priest and the Levite, he was a nuisance to avoid. But to the Samaritan he was a neighbor to love and help. Anyone who needs us is our neighbor—and to us Jesus says, "Go and do likewise."

ILLUSTRATION

A nurse escorted a tired, anxious young man to the bedside of an elderly man who was dying. "Your son is here," she whispered to the patient. The old man reached out his hand, and the young man wrapped his fingers around it, squeezing a message of encouragement. All through the night the young man sat holding the old man's hand and offering gentle words of hope. As dawn approached, the patient died. The young man placed on the bed the lifeless hand he had been holding, then went to notify the nurse. When the nurse began to offer words of sympathy to the young man, he interrupted her.

"Who was that man?" he asked. Startled, the nurse replied, "I thought he was your father." "No, " he answered. "I never saw him before in my life." "Then why didn't you say something when I took you to him?" asked the nurse. "I saw that he needed his son," he replied, "and his son wasn't here. When I realized he was too sick to tell whether or not I was his son, I knew just how much he needed me."

How to Conquer Greed

Luke 12:13-34

God wants us to overcome our greed and selfishness so we can put his purposes for our lives first. The story Jesus told in Luke 12 is acted out as regularly today as it was in Jesus' day. In this story, Jesus offers us some simple yet profound instruction on how to conquer greed.

We can conquer greed by making God's work our priority and trusting him to meet our needs.

I. WHAT'S SO WRONG WITH GREED?

A. According to the apostle Paul, "the love of money is a root of all kinds of evil. Some people, eager for money, have wandered from the faith and pierced themselves with many griefs" (1 Timothy 6:10).

B. Greed is the excessive desire to acquire or possess more material wealth than one needs. Greedy people are caught in an endless effort to satisfy their wants without ever reaching satisfaction.

C. The greedy man in Jesus' parable is described as selfish, having no thought for anyone but himself. He failed to acknowledge that God had blessed him and made his abundance possible. He was a man of confused purpose. He had no awareness of God's plan for his life—to be a steward of the great resources entrusted to him. He was, God said, a fool (Luke 12:20).

D. Greed causes us to pursue, clutch, and grasp at the visible to the neglect of the invisible. Our preoccupation with the sparkle and glitter of material things causes us to lose sight of the more important matters of the soul.

II. HOW DO I KNOW IF GREED HAS A GRIP ON ME?

Some of the symptoms of greed are

A. Obsessiveness. Luke 12:13 provides the setting for this parable: a man blurted out, "Teacher, tell my brother to divide the inheritance with me." In spite of the inappropriateness of interrupting Jesus' sermon, the man could not control himself. When our "wanter" is out of control, greed has set in.

B. Anxiety. Jesus gives express instructions not to worry about material things but to focus on what is really important (Luke 12:22).

C. Self-esteem tied to possessions. When we seek or derive our significance and approval from what we have, wear, drive, or the like, we are greedy (Luke 12:23).

D. Compromise for the sake of gain. Greed has set in when we set aside our values if they might cost us our wants.

E. Putting material things over spiritual things. Greedy people often sacrifice worship and service in the pursuit of more. Crowded schedules of daily life choke out time with God and time for God.

F. Loving things and using people. We should love people and use things. Practicing the opposite is a symptom of greed. When relationships become expendable in the desire for more of the material, greed has a grip on you.

III. HOW DO I BREAK FREE OF GREED?

A. Set your priorities to reflect life's real meaning and purpose. In Luke 12:31 Jesus calls us to seek his kingdom first. Give attention to that part of you "below the waterline," your soul.

B. Trust God to take care of your needs. Jesus also tells us not to be afraid, but to trust in him (Luke 12:32). Since God will take care of our real needs in life, we can hold our possessions loosely and even afford to be generous (2 Corinthians 9:6-8).

C. Make yourself rich toward God. In Luke 12:21 Jesus criticizes the rich man for not being "rich toward God," while in 12:33 he commands, "Provide purses for yourselves that will not wear out, a treasure in heaven." When we give to God, we are actually laying up treasure in Heaven.

CONCLUSION

Jesus is teaching us that it is possible that our preoccupation with things and our hope that they will bring contentment, pleasure, security, and self-worth can, in fact, cost us our very souls. We must be sure that greed does not have a grip on us. We must find our true source of satisfaction in God and invest our lives in ways that last and have eternal significance.

Made to Bear Fruit

Luke 13:1-9

Humans have a habit of pointing to the faults of others to make themselves appear better than them. This is what Jesus' audience for this parable was doing. By pointing out the tragic fate of the Galileans or those crushed by the Siloam tower, they were suggesting that they must be morally superior to those lost souls. Jesus, however, rejected their conclusion and reminded them that we are all equally guilty before God.

Only those producing the fruit of repentance will escape eternal punishment.

I. WE MUST REPENT OR PERISH.

A. The New Testament word for repentance, *metanoia*, means to turn from sin and to turn to God. The word originally had the idea of a complete change of one's mind, purpose, and feelings, leading to a new way of thinking and acting. Repentance is the unconditional surrender of ourselves to God and a complete commitment to his will and plan for our lives.

B. In Romans 6:3, 4, Paul says that becoming a Christian involves a death and a rebirth, a death to sin and a rebirth in Christ. That is why Paul later calls all believers to a new pattern of thinking and living (Romans 12:2).

C. In Luke 13 Jesus says we must repent or perish. God will not force us to follow him against our will. We can refuse God and his love. We can choose to be separated from him forever in Hell, a terrible monument to human freedom.

II. FRUITLESSNESS INVITES DISASTER.

A. According to Leviticus 19:23-25, fruit from newly planted trees was not eaten the first three years, and the fourth year the crops belonged to the Lord. So a farmer would not harvest any fruit for himself until the fifth year. But the man in the parable had been waiting for *seven* years for this tree to bear a crop of figs! The owner said, "Cut it down!" Uselessness invites disaster.

B. We must also be fruitful—our lives must show that the gospel has made a difference to us (Luke 6:44, 45). Being fruitful requires us to be connected to Jesus (John 15:5, 8; Galatians 5:22, 23; Colossians 1:10). While we are not saved *by* our works, we won't be saved *without* them.

C. I can't recognize many trees, but I know my fruits. I can't tell a Scotch pine from a Douglas fir or a Lombardy poplar from a rhododendron. But if you send me to the store for a bag of apples, I know better than to bring back a bunch of bananas. It's easier to recognize fruits than it is to identify trees.

III. WITH THE PRIVILEGE OF HEARING THE GOSPEL COMES GREAT RESPONSIBILITY.

A. When the vineyard owner wanted to cut down the fruitless tree, his gardener said, "Leave it alone for one more year, and I'll dig around it and fertilize it. If it bears fruit next year, fine! If not, then cut it down" (Luke 13:8, 9).

B. Knowing the gospel is a great privilege. It puts us in a favored position. But we also have a responsibility to do something with it. Mature Christians must "act their age." They must show good fruit for the years of Christian teaching they have received. In the same way, the seeker who hears the gospel can't pretend he didn't hear it. He must do something about it.

CONCLUSION

God is patient because he wants to give us opportunity to repent. As 2 Peter 3:9 reminds us, "The Lord is not slow in keeping his promise, as some understand slowness. He is patient with you, not wanting anyone to perish, but everyone to come to repentance."

This is an open-ended story. Did the tree ever bear fruit? Did the special care and attention the gardener gave it make a difference? Was the tree spared or cut down? We don't know what happened to the tree, but we can say what will happen to us.

ILLUSTRATION

Dante, in his *Divine Comedy*, tells of his journey into the world of the unseen. He was guided to those spirits who, like the penitent thief, had been sinners up to the last moments of their lives. But heeding the warning of Heaven, they had repented and were forgiven. Among them Dante is surprised to see one Buonconte, who had been sensuous, rebellious and vile while he lived on earth. How did he come to be among those who journey on to the vision of God?

Buonconte answers that, stricken in battle, he had fled away, leaving on the plain a gory trail from a gaping throat wound. As he lay dying, the minions of Hell came swooping down to bear him away, but God's angels had also come and stood on guard. The two forces debated for possession of his soul. So black was Buonconte's record that he believed himself forever lost. But just as the demons were claiming him for their own, an angel pointed to his eyelids, weighed down in the last long sleep, where hanging from their fringe was "one poor tear," a token of repentance. At the last moment he had turned his face toward God. Triumphantly the angels bore him to the realms of the redeemed.

I don't know about you, but I do not want to cut it that close. Repent now. Come to Christ now.

So, What's Your Excuse?

Luke 14:15-24

Jesus took so much pleasure in eating and drinking with his friends that the Pharisees accused him of being a glutton and a drunkard. However, Jesus' table fellowship was intended to symbolize for his companions the blessing of joyous fellowship in God's presence that will characterize the new age.

The Bible frequently uses the picture of a wedding banquet or great feast to describe both the present and future blessings of the Christian life. Jesus' parable of the great banquet in Luke 14 focuses on our responsibility to respond to God's invitation.

**Although everyone is invited to God's great banquet,
only those who accept his invitation may attend.**

I. GOD HAS PREPARED A GREAT BANQUET.

A. Luke 14:16 says, "A certain man was preparing a great banquet and invited many guests." The Christian life is a feast, not a funeral. Moreover, it is a "great" (Greek, *mega*) banquet. It is full of more love, joy, peace, hope, and meaning than this world can ever imagine.

B. The ultimate destiny and destination of every believer is the great "wedding supper of the Lamb" that will be held in Heaven (Revelation 19:9).

II. GOD HAS MADE EVERYTHING READY FOR THE FEAST.

A. Luke 14:17 states, "At the time of the banquet he sent his servant to tell those who had been invited, 'Come, for *everything is now ready.*'" By this we are reminded that salvation is God's work, not ours. It doesn't rest on what we *do* but on what Christ has *done.*

1. Jesus completely finished the work of our redemption on the cross. As 1 Peter 3:18 says, "For Christ died for sins *once for all,* the righteous for the unrighteous, to bring you to God."

2. Paul adds in Romans 4 that when we become Christians we are literally "credited" with the righteousness of Christ.

3. Don't think you have anything to wear to such a grand banquet? Then hear what Galatians 3:27 declares: "For all of you who were baptized into Christ have clothed yourselves with Christ."

B. Everything is ready. There is nothing more for you to do but accept God's invitation and come to the feast.

III. EVERYONE IS INVITED.

A. According to Luke 14:16, the banquet host "invited many guests." When some refused to come, he invited more (14:21). When there was still room at the table, the host said, "Go out to the roads and country lanes and make them come in, so that my house will be full" (14:23).

B. After Jesus returned to Heaven, when Peter opened the doors of the church on the Day of Pentecost, he promised the blessings of salvation to *all* who would receive Christ as their Savior (Acts 2:38, 39). Likewise, Revelation 7:9, 10 promises that the saved in Heaven will come "from every nation, tribe, people and language."

C. Finally, the Bible closes with these words in Revelation 22:17: "The Spirit and the bride say, 'Come!' And let him who hears say, 'Come!' Whoever is thirsty, let him come; and whoever wishes, let him take the free gift of the water of life."

IV. IT'S UP TO YOU TO ACCEPT OR REJECT THE INVITATION.

A. Unfortunately, Luke 14:18-20 notes that one man let his business keep him from the banquet. Another let his possessions keep him from the banquet. Another let his family keep him from the banquet.

B. Only those who accepted the invitation and came to the banquet enjoyed the feast. As is was then, so it is today.

CONCLUSION

Would you accept God's invitation to enter the kingdom of Heaven by accepting Jesus Christ as your Lord and Savior and being baptized (immersed in water) in his name? If you are already an immersed believer but not yet a member of this local church, would you accept our invitation to become part of God's family here? If you are a member, would you pray for and invite at least one family member, neighbor, or friend to come with you to church sometime in the next thirty days?

Everything is ready. The table is spread. The invitations have been issued. Come to the feast today!

ILLUSTRATION

Phillips Brooks told the story of Alexander the Great, who one day received a friend asking for money. The man asked for ten talents, but Alexander had fifty delivered to him. When the man returned and said that ten would be sufficient, Alexander replied: "Ten are sufficient for you to take, but not for me to give."

So it is with God's grace. God is generous to the utmost extreme, bestowing his grace freely on all who will receive it.

A Lost Boy
Comes Home

Luke 15:1, 2, 11-32

Luke 15 records the only time Jesus ever told three stories in a row to make the same point. Such emphasis on our Lord's part was not accidental, and we should not miss the importance of his message.

Every sinner has infinite value in the eyes of God.

I. LEFT TO OURSELVES, WE WILL BE LOST.

A. It didn't take the prodigal son long to throw away his life. Luke 15:13 says, "Not long after that, the younger son got together all he had, set off for a distant country and there squandered his wealth in wild living."

B. The lost boy's condition paints a vivid picture of what our lives are like in sin.
1. He put plenty of distance between himself and his father. He "set off for a distant country" (Luke 15:13).
2. He wasted his inheritance and had nothing to show for it in the end. He "squandered his wealth in wild living" (15:13).
3. He became a slave to circumstances. Luke 15:14, 15 states, "After he had spent everything, there was a severe famine in that whole country, and he began to be in need. So he went and hired himself out to a citizen of that country, who sent him to his fields to feed pigs." Romans 6:16 tells us that those who offer themselves to sin become slaves to sin.
4. He made himself miserable. "He longed to fill his stomach with the pods that the pigs were eating, but no one gave him anything" (Luke 15:16).

II. GOD LONGS FOR ALL OF US TO COME HOME TO HIM.

A. God loves us no matter how far we have gone or how long we have stayed away. Luke 15:20 reports, "But while he was still a long way off, his father saw him and was filled with compassion for him." (See also Ephesians 2:4, 5).

B. If we turn back toward God, his grace and love will quickly close whatever distance there was between us, as Jesus makes clear: "[the father] ran to his son, threw his arms around him and kissed him" (Luke 15:20).

C. God longs to bless us more than we deserve or can imagine (Luke 15:22-24).

III. NO ONE HAS A MONOPOLY ON GOD'S LOVE.

A. The self-righteous older brother was jealous and resentful of the love and grace the father showed to his brother.

1. He "became angry and refused to go in" to his brother's homecoming celebration (Luke 15:28).
2. He complained because their father wasn't throwing a party for him (15:29).
3. No one had implied that the younger son squandered his inheritance on prostitutes until the older brother made that accusation (15:30).
4. The older brother wouldn't even acknowledge the prodigal son as his brother but refers to him as "this son of yours" (15:30).

B. Proud, self-righteous, selfish people always feel they are not treated as well as they deserve. But the father was as tender and loving to the elder son as he was to the prodigal son.

1. Jesus' parable begins with the words, "There was a man who had *two* sons" (Luke 15:11).
2. The father "went out" to both sons (15:20, 28).
3. The father loved both sons. He reminded the elder brother, "You are always with me, and everything I have is yours" (15:31).

C. We never have to fear that we shall have less of God's love and favor if we share it with others.

IV. SAVING LOST PEOPLE IS AT THE TOP OF GOD'S AGENDA, AND IT OUGHT TO BE AT THE TOP OF OURS.

A. The night the lost son came home his father's house was filled with music and dancing. The father told the older brother, "We had to celebrate and be glad, because this brother of yours was dead and is alive again; he was lost and is found" (Luke 15:32).

B. The point of all three stories, the lost sheep (Luke 15:3-7), the lost coin (15:8-10), and the lost boy, is stated in Luke 15:10: "I tell you, there is rejoicing in the presence of the angels of God over one sinner who repents." God throws a party over every lost sinner who comes home to him. This is why evangelism is the centerpiece of our church's mission and should be the personal passion and responsibility of every member.

APPLICATION

The parable has an open-ended conclusion. Jesus does not say whether the elder brother ever responded to his father's invitation to join the party. Nor does he say how the younger son lived in response to his father's welcoming love. The Lord leaves it up to us to finish the story. Are you a lost child? Come home today. Are you already saved? Join your Father in welcoming your brothers and sisters into his family.